Concepts in Social Thought

Series Editor: Frank Parkin
Magdalen College, Oxford

Concepts in Social Thought

Citizenship

Rights, Struggle and Class Inequality

J. M. Barbalet

University of Minnesota Press

Minneapolis

Published by the University of Minnesota Press
2037 University Avenue Southeast, Minneapolis MN 55414
Published simultaneously in Canada
by Fitzhenry & Whiteside Limited, Markham.

Printed in Great Britain

Library of Congress Cataloging-in-Publication Number
88–27718

ISBN 0–8166–1775–9 (hardcover)
ISBN 0–8166–1776–7 (pbk.)

The University of Minnesota
is an equal-opportunity
educator and employer.

Contents

Preface

This book is concerned with the development of citizenship and its relationship with social institutions and processes, and especially social class. This is the ground occupied by T. H. Marshall (1893–1981) and most clearly though briefly expounded in his *Citizenship and Social Class*, first given in 1949 at Cambridge University as lectures to commemorate Alfred Marshall. The interest in Marshall's arguments has been growing steadily so that today it is almost impossible to pick up a sociology journal which does not contain an article with at least some reference to his work. It is inevitable therefore that Marshall and his critics should appear throughout the discussion to follow. Having accepted this limitation a book as short as this is forced to accept another: as the conceptual and theoretical issues are drawn from and confront Marshall and the literature generated around the discussion of his ideas, so the empirical discussion is largely confined to Britain.

This book was written during a busy teaching year and while I am alone responsible for its errors a debt of gratitude is owed to Margaret, who was engaged with her own writing, and to Tom, Felix and David, who never cease to be doing and talking, for their patience and loving support.

J. M. Barbalet

Theories of Citizenship

Citizenship is as old as settled human community. It defines those who are, and who are not, members of a common society. Citizenship is a manifestly political enterprise, yet two general questions arise out of its practice which show that an appreciation of only the political dimension is insufficient for a proper understanding of it. The issue of who can practise citizenship and on what terms is not only a matter of the legal scope of citizenship and the formal nature of the rights entailed in it. It is also a matter of the non-political capacities of citizens which derive from the social resources they command and to which they have access. A political system of equal citizenship is in reality less than equal if it is part of a society divided by unequal conditions.

In its own terms the practice of citizenship contributes to the 'public good'. But the structures in which citizens participate in their collective affairs have wider implications for the organization of society as a whole. Thus a second question raised by the practice of citizenship concerns the consequences of advances in citizenship rights, especially for the social relationships of citizens (and non-citizens) and for the social and economic institutions in which they live and work. In particular, disadvantaged groups in society might struggle for citizenship rights in order to improve their conditions. The question immediately arises of whether an expansion of citizenship participation can reduce class inequality, or affect the structure of relations between persons of different sex or race. These and similar questions guide discussion throughout this book.

The relationship between citizenship and social class is the focus of both the Marxist critique of bourgeois citizenship and the more recent analysis of it in the work of T. H. Marshall. Each of these positions is discussed in this first chapter which briefly surveys some influential theories of citizenship. The purpose of this chapter is not to answer questions so much as raise them. The issues for an understanding of citizenship indicated here will be more fully developed in the chapters to follow.

i

Citizenship can readily be described as participation in or membership of a community. Different types of political community give rise to different forms of citizenship. These simple principles were elaborated nearly two and a half thousand years ago in the third book of Aristotle's *Politics*. The chief difference between citizenship in the classical Greek city-state and in the modern democratic national state is the extent or scope of the political community in each. For Aristotle citizenship was the privileged status of the ruling group of the city-state. In the modern democratic state the basis of citizenship is the capacity to participate in the exercise of political power through the electoral process. Thus participation by citizens in the modern nation-state entails legal membership of a political community based on universal suffrage and therefore also membership of a civil community based on the rule of law. For Aristotle the status of citizenship was confined to the effective participants in the deliberation and exercise of power; today national citizenship extends across society.

The expansion of citizenship in the modern state is both the hallmark of its achievements and the basis of its limitations. The generalization of modern citizenship across the social structure means that all persons as citizens are equal before the law and therefore that no person or group is legally privileged. And yet the provision of citizenship across the lines dividing unequal classes is likely to mean that the practical ability to exercise the rights or legal capacities which constitute the status of citizen will not be available to all who possess them. In other words, those disadvantaged by the class system are unable to practically participate in the community of citizenship in which they have legal membership. The disability is a double one because in these circumstances citizenship rights which are only formal cannot influence the conditions which render the possession of citizenship ineffective, if not worthless.

The criticisms of modern democratic citizenship mentioned here were clearly outlined in the 1840s by Karl Marx in his study of the constitutions of the American and French Revolutions, through which modern citizenship first arose. Marx (1843: 219) summarizes his objections to modern democratic, or bourgeois, citizenship when he says that

> The state in its own way abolishes distinctions based on birth, rank, education and occupation when it declares birth, rank, education and occupation to be *non-political* distinctions, when it proclaims that every member of the people is an equal participant in popular sovereignty regardless of these distinctions, when it treats all those elements which go to make up the actual life of the people from the standpoint of the state. Nevertheless the state allows private property, education and occupation to act and assert their particular nature in their own way, i.e., as private property, education and occupation. Far from abolishing these factual distinctions the state presupposes them in order to exist.

Marx (1843: 221) does not wish to be understood as rejecting the achievements of modern citizenship, for he describes them as 'a big step forward' and as the best that could be achieved '*within* the prevailing scheme of things'. But this is precisely the point for Marx; he insists that mere *political* emancipation in citizenship is inadequate and instead advocates a general *human* emancipation in which persons are freed from the determining power of private property and its associated institutions. According to Marx, then, the limitations of citizenship which arises through political transformation can be overcome only through a social revolution in which the class basis of inequalities in social conditions and power is overthrown.

The alternative possibilities spelled out by Marx more or less constituted the parameters of political debate in nineteenth-century Europe. The choice seemed clear: either social inequalities were to be rendered irrelevant for membership in the status of citizen (the corollary of which is that citizenship could not modify or alleviate social inequality but in effect sanctioned or legitimated it), or social inequalities were to be abolished through social revolution. Yet political debate is never conducted with words alone, and in the course of any debate its terms tend to be redefined. The nineteenth-century debate on citizenship and revolution was fundamentally modified by the emergence of a labour movement which struggled for the right to form unions and the right to collectively bargain with employers over wages and conditions of work and employment. As a result of these struggles, either directly or indirectly, policies were developed which provided safety-nets against the effects of certain aspects of social inequality, and especially those connected with unemployment and old age. It will become clear in later chapters that the relationship between the labour movement and ameliorating policy is far from clear-cut. It is certain, though, that during the last hundred years or so the conditions of social inequality in Western capitalist societies have changed, and that these changes are associated with the participation of members of the propertyless and powerless class in the status of citizenship.

One type of response to this emerging situation has been to argue that changes in the social and economic circumstances of the working class have the effect of incorporating it in the structure of capitalism, thus undermining its revolutionary potential. Such arguments tend to assume that no modification is required of the account of citizenship outlined by Marx in 1843, say. We will see in later chapters that there is an element of truth in the idea of incorporation, although it is situated in a quite different context from that in which it is usually given. But even if the argument about working-class incorporation is accepted on its own terms, it would not follow that the concept of citizenship does not require re-examination. Precisely this point is implied when V. I. Lenin (1916: 117–8) shows that the advent of adult male suffrage in the development of political democracy means that the compliance of the working class can only be bought with social reforms. This arrangement, then, which Lenin calls 'Lloyd Georgism', is one in which citizenship, against Marx's earlier expectation, does in fact lead to certain changes in the structure of social inequality.

ii
Given the changes in the structure of social inequality brought about by developments in the concept and practice of citizenship, the question immediately arises of what these changes amount to. One approach, which has taken different forms and appeared in left- as well as right-wing guise, postulates a direct relationship between the advance of citizenship and the retreat of class. In effect Stanislaw Ossowski (1963: 184), for instance, summarizes this approach when he says that when changes in social structure are governed by political forces, as with developments of citizenship, then 'the nineteenth-century concept of class becomes more or less an anachronism, and class conflicts give way to other forms of social antagonism'. It is a big step indeed which reaches from the point that aspects of social inequality are affected by extensions in the

scope of citizenship, to the position that the class system itself is in decline. This approach tends to identify the class system with those disadvantages of class affected by the equalizing influence of citizenship. As systems of class inequality involve not only disadvantage but also privilege and the power to preserve it, it is unlikely that any changes brought to the class system through the development of citizenship, in which the powerful and privileged are included, would be fundamental. Against the ready acceptance of the decline of class is the argument that 'structures of social inequality . . . are inherently highly resistant to change' (Goldthorpe 1974: 218). Advances in the form of citizenship are likely to leave class structures intact, although class loyalty and class resentment may be affected by the removal of particular disadvantages. It should be clear that the question of the consequences of the development of citizenship on the structure of social inequality cannot be answered in the absence of a close re-examination of the issues involved.

Such a re-examination is encouraged by a critical reading of T. H. Marshall's *Citizenship and Social Class* (1950). In this work a theory of citizenship is formulated which focuses precisely on the relationship between developments in the nature of citizenship and in the class system. Marshall's argument is of particular interest because in explaining the nature of citizenship in post-World War II Britain, that is, since the rise of the welfare state, it also provides an account of the emergence of citizenship in the modern nation-state in terms of the historical development of capitalist society. Marshall argues that as capitalism evolves as a social system, and as the class structure develops within it, so modern citizenship changes from being a system of rights which arise out of and support market relations to being a system of rights which exist in an antagonistic relationship with the market- and class-systems. Marshall is able to advance this case by distinguishing between parts or elements of citizenship, and in doing so he offers a new characterization of citizenship which lends itself to an analysis of the relations between citizenship and society which is absent in other approaches.

The general understanding of citizenship in Marshall is entirely conventional. He says, firstly, that citizenship is a status attached to full membership of a community, and secondly, that those who possess this status are equal with respect to the rights and duties associated with it. Marshall (1950: 84) adds that different societies will attach different rights and duties to the status of citizen, for there is no universal principle which determines necessary rights and duties of citizenship in general. It is by going beyond the conventional idea that membership of a community is predominantly a political matter that Marshall is able to contribute to the study of citizenship. Three distinct parts or elements of citizenship are identified by Marshall which may or may not be present in any given constitution of citizenship: these are civil, political and social rights.

The elements of citizenship distinguished by Marshall are defined in terms of specific sets of rights and the social institutions through which such rights are exercised. The explicit acknowledgement of the requirement to understand citizenship in terms of rights and the institutional context through which rights are expressed is a genuine improvement on the idea that rights intrinsically attach to persons, and that the concept of 'human rights' in this sense can inform an understanding of the rights of citizens. Marshall's approach, on the other hand, indicates that rights are only meaningful in particular institutional contexts and are thus only realizable under specified material conditions. The three elements of citizenship identified by Marshall, in keeping with this perspective, have independent histories.

The civil element of citizenship is composed of the rights necessary for individual freedom, and the institution most directly associated with it is the rule of law and a system of courts. The political part of citizenship consists of the right to participate in the exercise of political power. Such rights are associated with parliamentary institutions. The social element of citizenship is made up of a right to the prevailing standard of life and the social heritage of the society. These rights are significantly realized through the social services and the educational system (Marshall 1950: 71–2). Marshall (1950: 74) adds that in the experience of the development of citizenship in the modern English nation-state the civil, political and social components developed in the eighteenth, nineteenth and twentieth centuries respectively. This should not be taken as indicative of an evolutionary assumption on Marshall's part, for he adds that this periodization should be 'treated with reasonable elasticity' and that these separate developments did in fact tend to overlap.

The principal point in all of this is that the different elements of citizenship have different institutional bases, and in significant respects different histories. This is to say that citizenship comprises elements which are not necessarily cut from the same cloth, and bear different relations with distinct social groups and with each other. These matters will be explored in the following chapter. All that is being established here is that Marshall offers a distinctive characterization of citizenship which allows us to see it in a new way.

It should be mentioned here that Marshall's approach to citizenship is novel not simply in stressing its distinct elements. Indeed, a germ of the idea that citizenship comprises three parts can be identified in a series of lectures given by Leonard Hobhouse at Columbia University in America in 1911, and subsequently published. Hobhouse (1928: 143) refers to political and civic inequalities in the principles of modern citizenship, and in discussing the Old Age Pensions Act of 1908 refers to the 'duty . . . of the community to provide the bare minimum necessary to an independent life' (1928: 175) and of a 'responsibility of the state for the individual' (1928: 184). The influence of Hobhouse on Marshall's thought is generally acknowledged, and was no doubt readily facilitated by the fact that Hobhouse was Professor of Sociology at the London School of Economics when Marshall first went there to teach in 1926. Marshall's more developed treatment of the elements of citizenship is not the same as Hobhouse's adumbration, certainly, but the lines connecting them are clear.

Where Marshall fundamentally departs from Hobhouse, and from liberal thought in general, is in the idea that not all citizenship rights are logically derivable from civil rights and especially property rights. Liberal theory holds that social rights, for instance, and also political rights are explicable in terms of the market rights of private property. These rights can be extended to persons in non-property classes when labour is regarded as the property of its possessor, as it has been in liberal theory since John Locke in the seventeenth century. Marshall has no need for such a teleology as he sees that while some rights might arise as a secondary product of other rights they can also attach directly and independently to citizenship as such (1950: 78, 111). In addition to this account of the basis of citizenship rights Marshall adds that the development of citizenship is not simply an outcome of the development of the state, as one finds in Hobhouse. According to Marshall (1950: 84, 92) changes in the nature of citizenship are achieved through conflict between social institutions and possibly between social groups. These ideas are not fully developed in

Marshall's discussion but they are widely held to be a real contribution Marshall has made to the theory of citizenship. They will be discussed in later chapters.

iii

Perhaps the most important aspect of Marshall's theory of citizenship is that it directly and explicitly addresses the question of the relationship between citizenship and social class. Marshall notes that the development of the institutions of modern citizenship in England coincided with the rise of capitalism. He regards this as anomalous because while capitalism creates class inequalities between those subject to it, citizenship is a status through which its members share equal rights and duties. Thus Marshall (1950: 84) concludes that it is 'reasonable to expect that the impact of citizenship on social class should take the form of a conflict between opposing principles'. Marshall's account of this relationship is particularly compelling because it is able to explain ostensibly opposite outcomes without itself being contradictory.

In the early phase of the development of capitalism citizenship tended to undermine the customary privileges of class which were a legacy of the feudal past, whilst at the same time it consolidated incipient capitalist class relations based on commodity production and exchange. During this period the class system was encrusted with hereditary privilege, customs and legal rights which derived from the earlier system of feudal estates. The development of modern citizenship, from the middle of the seventeenth century, entailing as it did an essential though limited element of legal equality, weakened and eventually undermined these aspects of class, and permitted the emergence of a class system based on a set of relations coterminous with the institutions of private property (Marshall 1950: 84–5). In undermining one type of class system citizenship promoted and secured a second. During the period of the eighteenth and nineteenth centuries the rights of citizenship were entirely harmonious with the class inequalities of capitalist society. According to Marshall (1950: 87) such rights were 'necessary to the maintenance of that particular form of inequality', because at that time citizenship rights were basically civil rights and civil rights 'were indispensible to a competitive market economy'. The reason for this is that civil rights bestow on those who have them the capacity to enter market exchanges as independent and self-sufficient agents. Capitalists and workers are indistinguishable from the perspective of civil rights in having the same right to enter into market exchanges and contracts with each other. If such rights are the core of citizenship, then citizenship will consolidate class inequalities.

When citizenship comes to incorporate political rights, and also social rights, then its relationship with the class system is more clearly conflictual than it is when it consists only of civil rights. The full potential danger to the capitalist class system from the political rights of citizenship was deflected during the nineteenth century in England only because the newly enfranchised working class was too inexperienced to effectively wield the political power provided by the nineteenth-century Reform Acts, according to Marshall (1950: 93). But this is not the end of the story, for while the working-class movement was not able to effectively mobilize political power during the closing decades of the nineteenth century, it created trade unionism as 'a secondary system of industrial citizenship parallel with and supplementary to the system of political citizenship' (Marshall 1950: 94). At this point the situation described by Marshall becomes especially complex, and particularly interesting. Trade unionism, and the collective bargaining with employers it permits, became a means by which the economic and social status of organized workers was raised. In other words, the collective exercise of rights by members of the working class in creating and using trade unionism established 'the claim that they, as citizens, were entitled to certain social rights' (Marshall 1950: 94).

The addition of social rights to the constitution of citizenship means for Marshall (1950: 84) that 'citizenship and the capitalist class system [are] at war'. It must be made clear that Marshall does not suggest that the war has had, or is likely to have, a fundamental outcome. Social citizenship has not destroyed class nor even in an unequivocal manner removed social inequality. Indeed, the development of citizenship, including social citizenship, has given rise to new inequalities (Marshall 1950: 106–8). What Marshall wishes to argue, though, is that social citizenship has tended to reduce certain social inequalities, and especially those associated with the operations of the market, so that the market value of individuals is no longer determinant of their real income because of the provision through state administration of economic goods and services as a right. Marshall (1950: 110) does not argue that class has been abolished by citizenship, but that citizenship 'has imposed modifications on' class. The precise nature of these modifications is subject to interpretation, certainly. It seems to be beyond dispute, though, that changes in the class system have been wrought through the exercise of citizenship rights by the working-class movement. The clear importance of Marshall's theory is that it readily identifies and explains these changes.

It will be evident from what has already been said that in Marshall's account of citizenship and social class is a theory of social change. He says that the growth of citizenship is 'stimulated both by the struggle to win those rights and by their enjoyment when won' (1950: 92). As the enjoyment of citizenship rights in their civil and political phases involves the exercise of liberty and political power, an element of potential conflict is inherent in the exercise and not simply in the origins of citizenship rights. This is especially so in a society divided by class inequalities in which citizenship rights are given to persons across class lines and in which the principle of citizenship and its components are opposed to class inequality. Marshall does not emphasize this aspect of citizenship, and it is not the only possible outcome of the relationship between citizenship and class. It does strongly suggest, though, that Marshall's approach to citizenship and social class entails not only that citizenship modify class, but also that class conflict is likely to be an expression of the struggle for rights and especially citizenship rights.

In summary then, Marshall sees the development of citizenship and of the class system in terms of the interactions between them. Through their antagonistic relationship citizenship and class inequality each contribute to changes in the other. Unlike most theorists of class structure Marshall recognizes the possible impact of citizenship on aspects of class inequality and therefore on class loyalty and class resentment, both of which tend to affect the nature and incidence of class conflict. Marshall sees such possibilities because he understands citizenship in terms not only of its legal and political dimensions, but also of its social component. It follows that from Marshall's perspective citizenship is not simply a status which detracts from class inequality but is in some tension with it, so that class conflict may possibly be about the nature and scope of citizenship rights. Any understanding of citizenship in the modern world, and in social and political theory, must therefore pay serious attention to Marshall's contribution.

iv

The preceding summary of *Citizenship and Social Class* indicates something of the range of issues it addresses. While the presentation here has simply attempted to condense Marshall's argument, it has also inevitably interpreted it. We will see that this interpretation is one of many. Donald MacRae (1974: 16) once remarked that Max Weber's fame as a classic sociological author rested on his ambiguity. This is not necessarily an unkind observation because a feature of any classic work must be that its meaning is enriched through re-reading. Ambiguity and richness can be different ways of describing the possibility of variable interpretation of a work. If this is indeed the essential criterion of a classic text then the treatment of Marshall by his interpreters will ensure the classic status of *Citizenship and Social Class*.

During the late 1950s and early 1960s *Citizenship and Social Class* exercised a considerable influence on sociological thought, and from the late 1970s to the present time there has been a revived interest in the work. In the literatures associated with these periods quite different, almost opposite, interpretations of Marshall's argument can be found, emphasizing certain aspects of it at the expense of others, and therefore in the least fortunate way revealing its complexity. The earlier interpreters of Marshall took him to be indicating a necessary integration of the working class into capitalist society through the development of citizenship and a subsequent decline of class and class conflict (Bendix 1964; Dahrendorf 1959). More recently, after relative neglect, possibly because the interpretations of the 1960s were taken for granted, Marshall has again become the subject of sociological interest, except that this time the idea that the systems of class and citizenship exist in tension with each other, and that the quest for citizenship might promote rather than reduce class conflict, has been emphasized (Giddens 1982; Goldthorpe 1978; Lockwood 1974; Turner 1986). Not all interpreters in the same period shared the prevailing view of Marshall, of course. S. M. Lipset (1964: xx) for instance, says that Marshall 'kept alive the perspective that society requires conflict'; and Barry Hindess (1987) tends to regard Marshall as a theorist of social integration rather than anything else.

Any interpretation which emphasizes one aspect of Marshall's argument at the expense of another is to that degree flawed. The strength of Marshall's theory is partly in its complexity, in its ability to proffer almost opposite possibilities without being contradictory.

Any interpretation which is adequate must capture this. The first thing to emphasize, then, is that in treating Marshall's argument in *Citizenship and Social Class* it is necessary to refer to all of the issues he treats, some of which have been mentioned above, and show their interconnectedness. The chapters which follow do this.

An aspect of all previous discussion of *Citizenship and Social Class* is its treatment in isolation from Marshall's sociological work as a whole. Some recent analyses of Marshall's arguments have introduced discussion of the concept of the 'hyphenated society' spelled out in his essay 'Value Problems of Welfare-Capitalism' and its 'Afterthought' (Marshall 1981). But with this exception it is almost as though Marshall wrote nothing of sociological interest apart from *Citizenship and Social Class*. In fact the idea that class and citizenship enter some form of antagonistic relationship in capitalist development, central to *Citizenship and Social Class*, runs through Marshall's sociological writing at least from his paper, 'The Nature of Class Conflict' (1938), to his latest work collected as *The Right to Welfare and Other Essays* (1981). Marshall's reputation as a sociologist justly rests with *Citizenship and Social Class*, but it is unfortunate that a large body of sociological writing which qualifies, clarifies and adds to it is largely unknown or at least untreated in the secondary literature.

The reasons for the neglect of Marshall's sociological writing apart from *Citizenship and Social Class* are not difficult to discover. In his brief review of Marshall's life and reputation A. H. Halsey (1984: 5–6, 8) notes that Marshall was a 'gentleman' by profession and – one is almost tempted to add, consequently – an 'amateur' as a sociologist (this in spite of the fact that Marshall held the Chair of Sociology at the London School of Economics from 1949 to 1956). Being a gentleman and amateur means detached and civilized observation, as opposed to, one presumes, partisan enthusiasm; and also elegant and economical writing free of technical terminology and copious citation, the trade marks of earnest professionalism.

But there is another dimension to Marshall's gentlemanly sociology, namely that his writing is what might be described as 'occasional'. Of the sixteen papers brought together in *Sociology at the Crossroads and Other Essays* (1963), the principal collection of Marshall's sociological writing, eleven were prepared and first presented as lectures, addresses, conference papers or contributions to symposia. In reading much of Marshall's sociology, then, one frequently comes across the invisible, and distracting, presence of the others who took part in the symposium or contributed to the conference. This tends to leave a sense of incompleteness concerning the paper at hand by Marshall. Thus one may be forgiven for feeling that Marshall's texts relate more to the occasion which gave rise to them than they do to each other and to the themes that they share.

Another aspect of Marshall's writing which may tend to discourage an interest in it in spite of the attention given to *Citizenship and Social Class*, again noted by Halsey, is that Marshall was not a system builder. This might lead to the view that no part of his output could illuminate another part of it. Marshall was not a system builder in the sense that he did not attempt to develop, for instance, a Weberian or a Durkheimian sociology, nor relate his particular endeavours to a clearly articulated general approach. Nevertheless, the arguments of *Citizenship and Social Class* do have a history in Marshall's thought, and this intellectual development can be traced in the prior and subsequent work.

The reasons for the neglect of Marshall's sociological writing are less important than the fact that it has a quality of thought and makes a substantive contribution which should be of lasting value to sociology, and is without influence only through neglect. Marshall has contributed to the theory of class, to the understanding of status, and to the analysis of post-war British society. We shall see that these contributions do in fact supplement and illuminate the treatment of citizenship and social class in his principal work. *Citizenship and Social Class* does have a context in Marshall's larger output and his other sociological writings enrich our understanding of his better-known arguments. Indeed, a highly appropriate way of consolidating and correcting other interpretations of Marshall is to treat the arguments of *Citizenship and Social Class* in conjunction with his associated writing. In this way the full complexity of the relationship between social class and citizenship will be more clearly and fruitfully revealed, as the following chapters will show.

After establishing the central place of Marshall in any serious discussion of citizenship and its relationship with the social structure it is essential to add that the chief purpose in reading Marshall is not simply to discover his strengths. One must begin with Marshall; but no progress can be made by remaining on the starting line. The discussion in the chapters which follow will show that a critical appraisal of Marshall is necessary and that in some crucial respects an alternative treatment of the connections between citizenship and social class has to be developed.

2

Citizenship Rights

Marshall (1950: 72) says that the civil, political and social rights which make up the separate elements of modern citizenship were 'wound into a single thread' under the feudal constitution. The amalgamation of feudal rights reflected the cohabitation of civil and political functions in feudal institutions. With the demise of estate society and the rise of market exchange unrestrained by customary, civic and religious precepts the economic and political spheres became institutionally separate and independent. As a consequence of this departure 'the institutions on which the three elements of citizenship depended parted company, [and] it became possible for each to go its separate way, travelling at its own speed under the direction of its own peculiar principles' (Marshall 1950: 73). The system of citizenship rights made up of relatively independent components with different constitutions and bases will be the focus of this chapter. The separation of the elements of citizenship is significant not only in terms of the analytical distinction between rights but also in the fact that the practices associated with each set of rights have quite different effects on social relationships and on the economic and political organization of society.

i

Before dealing with the separate components of citizenship it is necessary to say something about rights in general, what they are and why they are important. Citizenship can be characterized as both a status and a set of rights. This association of rights and status is not accidental. It will be shown here that the political importance of rights derives from the social nature of status.

In the most general terms rights are significant because they attach a particular capacity to persons by virtue of a legal or conventional status. That is, persons may have certain capabilities or opportunities for particular actions – certain powers – as a consequence of their status. A person's rights derive from their attachment to a status because in a meaningful sense one's status indicates what one can do, what capacities one has. To put it this way renders status an accomplished and achieved reality. This is an aspect of status which tends to predominate in its legal forms, for instance. Legally constituted rights, such as those of employees in industrial awards or of persons subject to criminal proceedings, are defined and enforced by public authorities. Legal rights, then, and the capacities they entail are provided to persons as a consequence of how they or their circumstances are categorized in the law, as a consequence of their legal status. It must also be said, though, that rights are created through being exercised, and that it is the exercise of rights which generates the capacities associated with them. This is as true of legal rights as any other and points to a further aspect of status as a social phenomenon.

'Status', Marshall (1954: 203) reminds us, 'emphasizes the fact that expectations (of a normative kind) exist in the relevant social groups'. These include expectations about appropriate behaviour not only from those who share a particular status but also from those who do not. The status of a particular category of persons is typified by how others relate to those in it. It is only when others come to accept a person's expectations as not only reasonable but legitimate that their status has any authenticity. To achieve the compliance of others in one's expectations can seldom be attained through persuasion alone. Perhaps this is why some writers have placed so much emphasis on the attainment of rights through struggle. The normative expectations of status not only sustain but are the mirror image of the rights and capacities attached to it. Thus, under certain circumstances, a *claim* to a right and not simply its legal establishment can attach capacities to persons in the generation and expression of a status.

It would be a mistake, however, to assume that status (and therefore rights) is simply achieved through struggle. It may be attained through struggle, certainly. But a status can be held only because it is publicly recognized as legitimate. In this sense the expectations, capacities and entitlements associated with a status and which therefore define social positions are a part of the very fabric of society. They possess a certainty, a naturalness and incontestability which social life requires and assumes. Rights therefore define for those who accept them the essential limits of social order, an ultimate boundary beyond which social existence itself is under threat. This, then, is a second aspect of the political importance of rights which is a consequence of the conventional nature of status.

It follows from what has been said here that any infringement of a right will be perceived by those involved as a uniquely serious matter. 'Rights', says Marshall (1950: 111), 'are not a proper matter for bargaining'. Directly associated with the idea that rights provide a minimum of social capacities and entitlements is the notion that the violation of a right is sufficient justification for the use of force in correcting the situation, for this latter is the ultimate recourse of 'society' defending itself. This, then, is a third aspect of the political importance of rights.

So far it has been shown that rights provide persons with capacities or capabilities and opportunities and that they can do so with a measure of security. This is because as attributes of status or position in society rights define an ultimate boundary and their contravention will be subject to sanction. This characterization raises a number of questions, especially issues of the relationship between rights and the distribution of social resources, power and interests.

Different rights attach different capacities to persons. Some rights, such as welfare rights which entitle persons to a minimum level of material well-being, provide access not simply to opportunities but also to conditions. The distinction between opportunity and condition is easy to make but the practical relation between them is complex. It is frequently remarked, for instance, that equality of opportunity leads to inequality of outcome or condition. This arises because abilities of one sort or another, or other means through which opportunities are taken, are themselves unevenly distributed through a population. 'A property right', Marshall (1950: 88) remarks, 'is not a right to possess property, but a right to acquire it, if you can, and to protect it, if you can get it'. Thus paupers and millionaires possess the same capacities through property rights without the distribution of property being in the least degree affected. The capacities exercised in the right to vote, however, or to strike, provide opportunities which are closer to the shaping of material conditions, and in the absence of such rights material conditions would be less likely to change in a direction favourable to those without social power. With some qualification, then, it is possible to say that certain rights (although not rights in general) may serve as a means to the social acquisition of material conditions which might not otherwise be available.

Since Thrasymachus' dialogue in the first book of Plato's *Republic* the idea that 'might is right' has enjoyed a good deal of currency. It is true that certain rights are means of organizing the interests of the powerful, property rights being a particular case in point. But it is necessary to add that rights are especially at issue when they provide capacities which simply would not otherwise be available. Rights are thus much more significant for those without social and political power than they are for the powerful. As we have seen certain rights provide access to opportunities and possibly to conditions that may otherwise be achieved only through the use of power. In this case rights are an alternative route to social resources and material conditions. Generally speaking this is why those who struggle for rights tend to see themselves as socially disadvantaged and powerless.

ii

Not all rights and not even all legal rights are citizenship rights. This may seem obvious but it is necessary to make the point forcefully because some confusion surrounds it. Bryan Turner (1986: 11, 100), for example, believes that the advent of rights for animals modifies the nature of citizenship. Marshall (1950: 81) on the other hand demonstrates that the provision of certain rights is precisely to compensate those who are excluded from the status of citizenship. Citizenship is a status bestowed on those who are full members of a national community, and citizenship rights, therefore, are those which derive from and facilitate participation in this 'common possession', as Marshall (1950: 92) calls it.

Citizenship rights, as the rights of persons in the community of a nation-state, will ultimately be secured by the state, but this is not their unique feature. Generally rights involve duties for any person exercising them. But certain rights exact duties from others. Citizenship rights impose certain limitations on the state's sovereign authority. In this vein H. R. G. Greaves (1966: 185) says that citizenship rights 'may be better called the duties of the state to its members'. Not all rights which constrain the state are *ipso facto* citizenship rights, but, as we shall see, all citizenship rights share this property. The different specific rights of citizenship do so in different ways, however. This partly explains why citizenship rights which are universal, and therefore in principle satisfy the interests of all who share them, in fact tend to serve distinct social interests and especially distinct social classes differently.

The different rights which are components of modern citizenship are not cut from the same cloth, and, under certain circumstances serious tensions may develop between them. Marshall tends not simply to underplay but to ignore this fact. This is because he is more interested in discussing the historical development of the three elements of citizenship than the relations between them. This is connected to a second point. As citizenship rights tend to be seen by Marshall as developing sequentially, so that civil rights, for instance, might sponsor other types of rights, the relationship between rights is assumed by him to be one of logical compatibility, if not entailment. Finally, in *Citizenship and Social Class* Marshall is concerned with the antagonisms between citizenship and social class rather than with the contradictions within citizenship itself.

Yet Marshall's exposition must raise a doubt about the coherence of modern citizenship. For instance he argues that not only are civil rights in citizenship compatible with capitalist inequalities, they are required for their maintenance (Marshall 1950: 87). He goes on to say that the political rights of citizenship, on the other hand, 'were full of potential danger to the capitalist system' (Marshall 1950: 93). And with the advent of social rights of citizenship the threat to the inequalities of market and class is most pronounced, according to Marshall (1950: 96–7). It is in this respect that there is at least a potential for practical incompatibility in the effects of the elements of citizenship. The possibility of this situation arising derives from differences in the principles and bases of the different elements of citizenship. This point can be demonstrated by a comparison of civil and social rights.

Civil rights include not only property rights and the right of contract but also rights to the freedoms of thought and speech, religious practice, and of assembly and association. They are in principle unified as civil rights in so far as each is a right permissive of human action. But they are more than this. In his 'Reflections on Power', Marshall (1969: 141) says that 'civil rights, though vested in individuals, are used to create groups, associations, corporations and movements of every kind'. In this sense, Marshall (1969: 142) continues, civil rights are 'a form of power'. In sharp contrast to civil rights, social rights, Marshall (1969: 141) says, 'are not designed for the exercise of power at all'. He goes on to say that while social rights are strongly individualistic, they refer 'to individuals as consumers, not as actors'. Ontologically the difference between civil and social rights could not be greater.

It was mentioned above that citizenship rights constrain the state. As elements of citizenship both civil and social rights do this, but in different ways. This fact is nicely captured in C. B. Macpherson's (1985: 23) statement that civil rights are rights *against* the state whereas social rights are claims for benefits guaranteed *by* the state. This distinction highlights the difference between civil and social rights from the perspective of the state's obligations to its citizens. For persons to *act* as citizens there must be freedoms the state cannot invade and therefore actions which the state cannot perform; for persons to *consume* as citizens the state must provide, and is therefore obliged to perform certain specific actions. This distinction raises a further difference between the two types of rights. The provision of benefits by the state means that social rights require not only an extensive administrative apparatus but also certain conditions of expertise and professionalism in the delivery of social benefits (Marshall 1975: 206) which are unnecessary in the practice of civil and political citizenship. A corollary is that in addition to the costs of the social benefits themselves social rights in citizenship tend to generate a stratum of administrative, semi-professional and professional workers who are not insignificant in the class, fiscal and political structures and processes of modern democracies. There is no parallel social effect of civil rights.

A demonstration that two things are different could not itself lead to the conclusion that they are opposed. Under certain circumstances, however, civil and social rights do find themselves in antagonism. The constraint exercised by social rights against the state is direct and imposes costs on the state and therefore taxes on citizens. There is therefore a structural budgetary basis for a potential threat to social rights. And the nature of social rights, as those of consumers rather than actors, means that they are necessarily vulnerable. During periods of economic decline there may arise a contradiction between the need for the maintenance of the institutional basis of social rights through taxation and the requirements of capital accumulation. At such times a pressure against social rights may take the form of a reassertion of civil rights, not simply as property rights (although that is not insignificant) but as an independent source of economic action and power. Marshall's

(1950: 87) comment that civil rights were essential to a competitive market economy because they gave to each person 'the power to engage as an independent unit in the economic struggle' is followed by his observation that for this reason civil rights 'made it possible to deny social protection on the ground that [a person] was equipped with the means to protect himself'. Recent developments in advanced capitalist societies have given these notions a new voice.

It would be imprudent to assume that the different component rights of modern citizenship are equally guaranteed by the state. Not only are civil and social rights founded on different principles and bases, they may exist in some tension with each other. This situation is complicated further by the different involvement of distinct sectors of the state in the operations of citizenship rights. Ralph Miliband (1984: 118–9) makes this very point when he mentions that the courts have traditionally attempted to annul or at least limit the scope of industrial rights granted by Parliament. What has been described here as tension between the different rights of citizenship has led Nigel Young (1967: 6) to suggest that the concept of citizenship is essentially artificial in so far as it postulates the articulation of elements of a unity which are in reality contradictory and antithetical. This conclusion is too extreme. That social institutions manifest internal tensions does not signify their impossibility but that they function in an unequal society in which tensions are unavoidable.

It will be clear that the threat to social rights from civil rights in the example given above is ultimately a class threat. While citizenship rights can be exercised by all who possess them, they in fact tend to serve members of different classes differently. Marshall was well aware that civil and social rights each have a clear class bias in their principles and operation. But he failed to seriously consider the logical relationship between rights, and the associated problem of the propensity of the state to defend the different elements of citizenship unequally. Certain civil rights are central to the foundations of capitalist economies and their operation. For these reasons they have the potential to undermine social rights.

In focusing on the serial development of citizenship in which the support of one right was provided by another Marshall tends to emphasize a quite different aspect of civil rights, although just as important as the one just mentioned, namely their role in the development of the working-class movement and its political and industrial opposition to aspects of capitalism.

iii

The full complexity of the relationship between the elements of citizenship can be most clearly demonstrated in a discussion of industrial rights. Questions of the role of civil rights in the formation of and their relationship with other rights, of class bias in citizenship rights, and of the constituting elements of modern citizenship, are all raised by the concept of industrial citizenship and Marshall's treatment of it.

Towards the end of *Citizenship and Social Class* Marshall (1950: 122) refers to the 'present phase of the development of democratic citizenship' in a manner and context which suggests that he believes a subsequent phase is imminent. Indeed, his discussion of the development of citizenship in which new political and then social elements are added to civil rights conveys more that there has been an historical progression of phases of development than that the development must be limited to the evolution of only these three components and no more. Certainly this is how others have interpreted Marshall. Ralf Dahrendorf (1973: 410–1), for instance, in a brief comment on Marshall's work, refers to the 'gradual expansion of citizenship from the legal to the political and social sphere', and adds that this process 'is still unfinished' as 'new dimensions of citizenship' may be discovered by political organizations and social groups. It is particularly odd, then, that 'industrial rights' are mentioned by Marshall in his account of the development of modern citizenship, but are not included by him as an authentic component of citizenship along with civil, political and social rights.

Marshall's discussion of industrial rights is briefer and less clear than his treatment of civil, political and social rights. Industrial rights, the rights of employees to form trade unions, to collectively bargain and to strike, are ostensibly treated by him as civil rights. It is this characterization of industrial rights to which Anthony Giddens (1982: 172) takes strong exception. His argument rests on the assumption that rights might be distinguished by their class bias. The rights of individual freedom and equality before the law were fought for and won by the rising capitalist class against feudal privilege and restrictions on commerce, according to Giddens. Their importance to the bourgeoisie, he continues, was to strengthen the power of employers over their workforce. The rights to form unions and strike, on the other hand, were not simply extensions of existing civil rights, Giddens argues, but were achieved in struggle by the working-class movement against the resistance of employers and the state. Thus Marshall's inclusion of industrial rights with civil rights in general is not convincing to Giddens.

Whilst Giddens' conclusion about the independent status of industrial rights in modern citizenship is entirely acceptable, and will in fact be developed below, his arguments are not adequate. It is true that Marshall treats industrial rights as though they emerged gradually through the enlightened development of market institutions, a position which has to be rejected as quite misleading. But Giddens is wrong to distinguish the civil rights of bourgeois liberties from the industrial rights of labour unions on the grounds of who fought for what. Not only was the involvement of the lower and working classes crucial in winning bourgeois freedoms in mid-eighteenth-century England during the 'Wilkes and Liberty' struggles, but precisely these freedoms, of the press, of opinion and of assembly, were central to the struggle for trade unionism and the right to strike, and therefore essential to the emergence of industrial citizenship.

Marshall's discussion of industrial citizenship is not entirely what it appears to be; it is necessary to go through it carefully to see exactly what it claims. The obvious point is that Marshall (1950: 93) saw the nineteenth-century advent of collective bargaining as a strengthening of civil rights rather than the creation of a new right. But the contradistinction here is not between civil rights and industrial rights but between civil rights and social rights. Collective bargaining requires an acceptance of market exchange but modifies the units entering the exchange so that associations or combinations of workers rather than individual workers enter into agreements over wages and conditions with employers. Marshall's point is that this development was a means of strengthening the hand of labour and thus securing minimum conditions for workers through the market place, rather than asserting a basic right to minimum wages and conditions. But this situation was entirely transitional because the collective use of civil rights was, according to Marshall (1950: 94), precisely to 'assert basic claims to the elements of social justice'. During the twentieth century these claims have become accepted as full and genuine rights of social citizenship.

The instrument through which civil rights were used to establish social rights, as Marshall puts it, was trade unionism. Marshall's (1950: 93-4) argument is that trade unions exercised the civil rights of their individual members collectively. He adds, though, that this is entirely anomalous, for civil rights, Marshall (1950: 93) says, 'were in origin intensely individual'. With the more recent develop- ments of incorporation, though, collectivities are 'enabled to act legally as individuals'. The difficulty, however, is that trade unionism has developed and functions by avoiding incorporation. Trade unions, Marshall (1950: 93–4) says, can

> exercise vital civil rights collectively on behalf of their members without formal collective responsibility, while the individual respon- sibility of the workers in relation to contract is largely unenforceable.

The absence of the correlative civil duties should have alerted Marshall to the fact that trade unions do not exercise collective civil rights, but rights of a different kind. We shall return to this point below.

Marshall (1950: 94) does not leave the matter here but goes on to argue that 'the acceptance of collective bargaining was not simply a natural extension of civil rights.' It is, he continues, a 'transfer' of certain important processes 'from the political to the civil sphere of citizenship'. And yet, Marshall interjects, 'transfer' is not an appropriate term, for at this time workers either did not possess or did not know how to use the political right of the franchise. Marshall (1950: 94) wishes to describe the situation more accurately as one in which trade unionism has 'created a secondary system of industrial citizenship parallel with and supplementary to the system of political citizenship'. Here is Marshall's argument about industrial citizenship: it is a secondary system of citizenship, based on the institution of trade unionism, which is responsible for collective bargaining as a means not so much of seeking market equilibrium as of laying claim to certain basic rights of social justice.

Apart from this brief description of industrial citizenship as a secondary right, the concept of secondary rights is mentioned elsewhere in *Citizenship and Social Class* only in a discussion of nineteenth-century political rights. Marshall (1950: 78) argues that while citizenship in nineteenth-century England did not have a political component, because the electoral franchise was the privilege of a limited economic class, it did not follow that citizenship at this time was politically meaningless. At this time no citizen, apart from the insane and the criminal, was excluded by personal status from voting in elections. The civil rights of citizenship entitled men to enter the market and purchase property or rent a house, and to take advantage of any political rights which went with such economic achievements. Thus nineteenth-century citizenship 'did not confer a right', according to Marshall (1950: 78), 'but it recognized a capacity'. In this sense nineteenth-century political rights were a 'secondary product of civil rights'. In the twentieth century, of course, this situation no longer obtains and political rights are attached 'directly and independently to citizenship as such'. In this account civil rights have a role only in the historical origins of political rights, but no relevance for an understanding of their function and operation.

Given the analogous secondary nature of political and industrial rights in the nineteenth century, could not what Marshall says of political rights in the twentieth century also be said of industrial rights? Marshall seems to think not, but his arguments are highly tendentious. Marshall (1950: 112) holds that whereas in the past trade unionism asserted social rights by 'attacks delivered from outside the system in which power resided', from the mid-twentieth century 'it defends them from inside, in cooperation with government'. This defence of citizenship rights by something like a joint discussion of policy by the unions and the government, which until recently characterized the British political scene, carries with it corresponding duties, according to Marshall. An appreciation of these duties includes what he calls a 'lively sense of responsibility towards the welfare of the community'. The mark of irresponsibility in this context is a high incidence of unofficial strikes – unofficial because of the breach between trade union leaders who understand and accept their responsibility and the rank and file who do not. The implication of Marshall's account is that with the political incorporation of trade union leaders industrial citizenship, which existed in the nineteenth century as a secondary system of rights 'supplementary to the system of political citizenship', is in the twentieth century rendered redundant. Marshall's grounds for believing this are questionable, and his general characterization of industrial citizenship dubious.

It is of interest that Marshall (1950: 112) accepts that strikes will be justified by those who engage in them through an appeal to the 'status rights of industrial citizenship'. As we saw at the beginning of this chapter and in Marshall's observation above, the recognition of a capacity is the recognition of a right which, if not conferred as such, may function as a secondary right of citizenship. But in addition to the claims of strikers it is possible to point to a body of legislation in all advanced capitalist countries which in fact does confer industrial rights. These are not equivalent to or logically connected with social rights, as Marshall suggests, although they have been used to defend the social and economic conditions of trade unionists and their families before social rights had been put in place. Industrial rights are not individualistic, obligatory, or consumption-orientated but the rights of individuals permitting (and perhaps enabling) their collective action and organization. The institutional bases of industrial rights are trade unions and similar associations of employees. Industrial citizenship is a status limiting the commodification of persons in employment and therefore includes the right to influence the terms of employment, the conditions of work and the level of pay, and is therefore also the right to develop and sustain the independent means of achieving these things through the organization of combinations or unions.

Industrial rights share with civil rights a permissive quality and an enabling capacity, but the suggestion of Reinhard Bendix (1964: 80), for instance, that the industrial right to combine is more or less continuous with the civil right of association ignores crucial differences between them. Individual rights are paramount in civil citizenship, and any collective action can only be justified as an expression of civil rights if the right of the individual in them is preserved. This requirement extends to the correlative duties and responsibilities of civil rights which attach to the individual partici- pants in unincorporated collectivities or to the artificial corporate individuals. These conditions do not necessarily obtain in the case of industrial rights.

Trade unions can only function properly if the rights of their individual members are subordinate to the rights of the collectivity, and in their operations they frequently infringe the rights of property and contract by preventing manufacture and trade through strike action. Even when routinely influencing wages and conditions, the exercise of industrial rights modifies property rights by encroaching on the prerogatives of management. Thus the exercise of industrial rights may be injurious to the civil rights of individual workers, possibly including trade unionists, and employ- ers alike. Unless this is accepted and accommodated in law, industrial rights are without legal sanction and industrial citizenship will remain a secondary system of rights. In the history of British unionism the legislation of 1871 and 1896, which recognized the legality of unions, was useless in protecting industrial rights until the passage of the Trade Disputes Act of 1906. Industrial citizenship in

Britain can be dated from the 1906 legislation, which declared that a trade union could not be sued 'in respect of any tortious act alleged to have been committed by or on behalf of a trade union', and removed it from civil conspiracy, breach of contract and prevention of picketing restraints (Brown 1983: 38–9). Industrial rights are not only distinct from civil rights but in their application may be opposed to them.

Given the obvious class bias of industrial rights their incorporation in citizenship may appear problematic. Although in practice industrial rights directly serve one class, and, it could be added, potentially injure members of another class, they remain universal. They do not require that everyone be an employee, but offer some protection against commodification to all those who find themselves in the employment of another. In this respect industrial rights are entirely analogous to property rights. They are universal in being available to all who through their material situation need to draw upon them. But there is another aspect to industrial rights which clearly brings them into the orbit of citizenship. Industrial rights are used by organized workers against employers. But in doing so they follow set limits for the purpose of common participation in a unified functional system. In this sense industrial rights are premissed on what Marshall (1950: 92) calls a 'loyalty to a civilization which is a common possession'. It is arguable that in the absence of industrial rights the vast mass of employees would not be able to partake in the industrial civilization of modern capitalism. It is partly in recognition of this fact, and partly because under certain circumstances industrial citizenship may tend to serve certain interests of employers, that a consensus exists which consolidates the citizenship status of industrial rights.

iv
It will be clear that the relationship between the different components of citizenship is complex. Civil rights, for instance, are crucial in the foundation of the capitalist economy, but also provide opportunities for workers to challenge aspects of it. Industrial rights tend to oppose aspects of civil rights and especially the property and contract rights of employers; but in helping to maintain and expand wages and provide security in employment, they tend also to stabilize commodity markets and industrial relations. The logical relationship between different types of rights is connected with and in part reflects the social relations found in society at large.

Rights are important in social analysis not because they structure social relationships – if rights do this at all they do it incompletely – but because people struggle to achieve and defend rights which they believe will provide minimum opportunities and therefore conditions for social existence, and because rights (especially citizenship rights) are associated not simply with social status but with social institutions which are at the core of social structure. It is these institutions, which have imperfect relations with rights, which tend to structure social relationships.

It does not follow from these remarks that analysts can form an impression of social relationships and interests simply by knowing what rights are accepted in a community. The relationship between different rights is complex and varies with changes in circumstances. Also, rights are not determinants of action so much as resources which actors might draw upon. This is implicit in the idea that rights entail capacities attached to a status. So while rights do not dispose persons to particular courses of action – material circumstances are more likely to do that – rights tend to facilitate social actions in various ways. In this sense rights are integral to the social fabric, and any social analysis which has no place for an understanding of the significance of rights and especially citizenship rights is that much the poorer.

3

The Rise of Citizenship

Current discussion of the development of citizenship points in opposite directions. On the one hand citizenship is seen as an expansive sphere in which new rights are added to a growing body of rights as new social forces are included in the national community. On the other hand there is the idea that the exercise of citizenship rights can never be guaranteed and is often precarious. Recent trends in Western capitalist societies have led Anthony Giddens (1982: 177), for instance, to argue that Marshall's evolutionary account of the development of citizenship ignores the fact that we 'cannot suppose . . . that the battle for civil and political rights has been won'. In a complementary vein Bryan Turner (1986: 64) has emphasized the 'contingent' nature of the process through which citizenship develops, and cautioned that such a development has 'no necessary historical logic or unfolding process'.

It is true that a new development of citizenship might come to threaten established interests, and that these in turn could attempt to shrink the practice of citizenship back to earlier limits. But it is difficult to believe that any assault on citizenship rights could be total, except through revolution. While the operation of citizenship rights is ever subject to contemporary influences, the advent of the institutions of citizenship and their consolidation have a clear historical reality, a reality which must play a role in the continuing development of rights. It follows that the career of citizenship is indeed contingent, but also that it has a history which unfolds through time. And while the course of history is never logically pre-determined, it is set by social conditions and determinants. This chapter will indicate what have been the principal social conditions and determinants in the historical rise of modern citizenship.

i

One well-established approach to the historical development of rights holds that democratic citizenship arises out of the evolution of industrialization, or from the civic progress of nations. More recent historiography, on the other hand, emphasizes the role of the contest of interests, of struggle, compromise and containment, in the extension of citizenship rights to previously excluded groups, and especially the working class. Marshall's place in relation to these approaches is surprisingly ambiguous. Bryan Turner (1986: 60) says that 'Marshall can be interpreted as saying that social violence has the potential for expanding the universalistic definition of the citizen', whereas Anthony Giddens (1982: 171) claims that Marshall 'fail[ed] to emphasize that citizenship rights have been achieved in substantial degree only through *struggle*'. Other commentators tend to support Turner's interpretation against Giddens'. S. M. Lipset (1964: xx) says that Marshall 'kept alive the perspective that society requires conflict', and A. H. Halsey (1984: 11) maintains that 'Giddens' criticism cannot be fully sustained when . . . Marshall describes class and citizenship as principles or social forces which have been "at war in the twentieth century" and this conflict of principles "springs from the very roots of our social order" . . . Marshall saw conflict . . . as a permanent and indeed desirable feature of a dynamic society'. We shall see how misleading a consensus of interpretation can be.

Marshall (1950: 92) does say that the growth of citizenship is stimulated 'by the struggle to win those rights'. But he goes on to add, virtually in the same breath, that the 'familiar instruments of modern democracy were fashioned by the upper classes and then handed down, step by step, to the lower'. The struggle which Marshall refers to here is not necessarily social struggle, between groups or classes of people, but principally struggle against established ways of doing things. Elsewhere, of course, Marshall (1950: 84, 122) refers to conflict, as Lipset and Halsey indicate; this is a conflict between the opposing principles of citizenship, on the one hand, and class or capitalist society, on the other. Use of the term 'conflict' in this context however, is ambiguous and misleading. Marshall's discussion of conflict here does not point to social struggle and certainly not social violence, for these latter refer to a particular type of relationship between social actors. The conflict which Marshall refers to is between sets of institutions or the parts of a social system, as opposed to the actors within it (see Lockwood

1964). Giddens (1979: 131) has shown, in a quite different context, that the term 'conflict' properly refers only to struggle between actors or groups expressed as actual social practices, whereas the term contradiction should be used to refer to the disjunction of structural principles of system organization. Marshall's conflict is more contradiction than struggle.

The conflict of principles to which Marshall refers is precisely the contradiction between the equality of status in citizenship on the one hand and the inequality of class in market society on the other. As we saw in the previous chapter, this conceptualization encourages the view that citizenship develops through the rise of secondary rights on the basis of civil rights. While civil rights are entirely compatible with class inequalities, the political and social rights (the origins of which are as secondary rights of civil citizenship) are opposed to class inequality. Thus the development of citizenship is through the conflict, or more properly through the opposition and contradiction between the principles of citizenship and of class. This account does not itself address the question of whether the relationship between social groups caught up in this process will be antagonistic. Marshall's comments on this matter are too few to permit a conclusive interpretation, but the bias of his account seems to be toward bargaining and conciliation rather than social conflict and struggle or violence.

Marshall's account in *Citizenship and Social Class* is primarily concerned with the effect of the development of citizenship on the structure of class inequality. Some writers have seen in Marshall an explanation of the rise of citizenship. To the degree that one exists it has more in common with the now discredited view that citizenship develops as national civic progress expands than with any other. An explanation of the development of citizenship in terms of the application of existing rights in the creation of new ones is incomplete if it fails to indicate the facilitating conditions under which such things occur and the social groups involved. It is for this reason that an account of the social determinants in the historical development of citizenship is not particularly assisted by a reading of Marshall.

ii

Discussion at various points in the previous chapters suggests that rights are not given so much as won. By the end of the present chapter it will be clear that these are not entirely alternative possibilities; but a conception of the *struggle* for rights does inform the current sociological perspective on their development. It is therefore with the struggle for rights that we begin. As Giddens (1982: 171) puts it, the 'extension of citizenship rights, in Britain as in other societies, was in substantial degree the result of the efforts of the underprivileged to improve their lot'. He goes on to explain that in order to attain citizenship groups previously excluded from its scope have had to struggle against the resistance of those who have been opposed to its extension. Such struggle does not occur in a vacuum, and striving for a goal does not imply that it will be achieved. It is necessary therefore to identify the conditions under which struggle for citizenship rights might succeed.

Modern or democratic citizenship has a history which parallels the growth of Western capitalism. But citizenship rights do not simply arise out of capitalist tendencies themselves. Industrialization, the creation of a propertyless working class, the formation of a professional middle class, and the development of scientific technologies can all occur without requiring or creating civil, political, social or any other types of citizenship rights. Nevertheless capitalist development has tended to create a social structure and especially a class structure which provides elements of the necessary context in which democratic citizenship might arise.

The first thing which should be mentioned as relevant to this consideration, and which is most frequently neglected, is the way in which capitalist development is likely to remove from the social structure class forces which would otherwise inhibit the progress of modern citizenship. In particular the rise of capitalist relations through the commercialization of feudal agriculture began a process which displaced the peasantry from the social and political landscape. This tendency was given added impetus in England by the Civil War of the 1640s and the parliamentary enclosures of the eighteenth century. According to Barrington Moore (1969: 21) the Civil War 'eliminated the king as the last protection of the peasantry against the encroachment of the landed upper classes.' Moore (1969: 28) goes on to say that the enclosures served the interests of the larger landlords and 'broke the back of the English peasantry, eliminating them as a factor from British political life'. The destruction of the peasantry was crucial for the development of bourgeois democracy, and therefore for modern citizenship, because it eliminated a 'huge reservoir of conservative and reactionary forces' (Moore 1969: 30). Societies in which a large peasantry remained significant in the class structure, such as Germany and Japan, failed to achieve modern democratic citizenship through internal processes as a consequence.

A further aspect of the commercialization of English agriculture, but one which refers to more positive outcomes of capitalist development for the rise of modern citizenship, is that during the eighteenth and nineteenth centuries the hereditary landed upper class shared common capitalist interests with the rising industrialists of the period. In more general terms it can be said that capitalist development creates competitive intra-ruling class relationships within the context of a unified sovereign state (Therborn 1977: 33). In the early stages of capitalist development and by the eighteenth century these things were associated with the development of civil rights as the core of an emerging national citizenship. By the nineteenth century competition within the ruling class, especially between landed and urban capital, had led to a parliamentary rivalry for popular electoral support. This division within the unity of the ruling class for appeal to a wider public not only led to the Factory Acts of the 1840s, with the landed interests supporting pressure from labour against the manufacturers, but also to the extension of the franchise through the 1867 Reform Act in an attempt to increase the parliamentary power of the Tories over the Liberals. This same ruling class configuration, of rival parties seeking mass support, led to the pioneering social legislation of 1908–11 (Middlemas 1979: 41–2). In other words, the structure of intra-ruling class competition, which tends to be sponsored by capitalist development, provides a necessary context for the creation of modern citizenship and its expansion.

It will be clear from the above account that modern citizenship in England can be described, as Marshall describes it, as moving through three stages in which the civil element is established by the eighteenth century, and the political and social elements are added in the nineteenth and twentieth centuries. Giddens' (1982: 173) disagreement with this chronology, insisting that civil and political citizenship rights developed together, derives from a confusion between power and rights. Civil rights in citizenship consolidate capitalist relationships, as we have seen Marshall indicate, and therefore capitalist class power. But political citizenship, being rights of political participation without limitation by economic status, could only be added to the general status of citizenship when a class emerged in the social structure which was prepared and able to fight for such rights. This of course is Giddens' more general point; but it too requires qualification.

A third aspect of capitalist social structure, then, which serves as a condition under which modern citizenship might develop, is the rise of the working-class movement. Göran Therborn (1977: 34) argues that the positive tendencies of competitive capitalism have not themselves led to democracy; rather it has been the basic contradiction between the classes of capital and labour which has promoted the rise of democracy beyond the dominant class and its immediate supporters. In recognizing the importance of the rise of the working class as a condition for the development of democratic citizenship, Therborn offers three very important qualifications. The first is that pressure from the working class has never directly led to the gaining of citizenship rights 'in the heat of battle'. Therborn (1977: 29) goes on to say that the common pattern is for the dominant class to initially resist pressure for reform, and to offer concessions only after a period of such resistance. Not only are working-class struggles for democratic citizenship never directly or immediately successful, they are seldom successful by themselves. This is Therborn's (1977: 24) second point, namely that the labour movement has never been 'strong enough to achieve bourgeois democracy on its own, without the aid of victorious foreign armies, domestic allies more powerful than itself, or splits in the ranks of the [class] enemy.' The third point Therborn (1977: 34) raises is that while protracted struggle in alliance with others may lead to an expansion of citizenship, the initiative has always rested with the dominant class, so that 'the critical questions of timing and form – of when and how democracy was to be introduced' have never been the prerogative of those struggling for rights. We shall return to these matters in later chapters. The point to emphasize here is that it is insufficient to point merely to struggle as the basis of rights because the outcome of such struggle must be understood in terms of a larger context.

Whilst an appropriate class structure is necessary for the development of modern citizenship, it is itself an insufficient platform for it to rise from. Other facilitating conditions are required. The most obvious is a material basis of economic prosperity. In the context of a world-dominant and expanding capitalist economy demands for reform placed on the English state have historically been relatively easy to accommodate. In his explanation of the rise in democracy in England Moore ties this to the fact that the repressive capacity of the English state was underdeveloped. Moore (1969: 32) argues that the relative weakness of the state repressive apparatus in England, a legacy of the Civil War, the evolution of the Monarchy, and England's island form leading to reliance on a navy rather than an army, meant that non-repressive means were used to ameliorate and control expressions of discontent. This was possible largely as a consequence of national economic prosperity and well-being. In economically less favourable circumstances, such as those of nineteenth-century Germany, popular discontent led not to political and economic reform but to forceful repression. It needs to be added here that the relationship between state repression and citizenship rights will almost certainly always be negative. For instance commentators frequently notice that the exercise of military force in Northern Ireland is part of a process which threatens civil rights in Britain.

Another important although frequently ignored factor in any account of the expansion of national citizenship is the condition of the international order. Dominant classes and political states which feel themselves to be at risk and under threat from foreign powers are not likely to grant concessions and reforms at home. On the contrary, any struggle for new rights under such circumstances is likely to lead to repression. The 'red scares' of 1919–20 in the United States of America, a reaction justified by antipathy to the communist revolution in Russia, were directed against civil rights, political dissent and industrial citizenship. Much earlier and in many ways more serious, the effect of the French Revolution on the development of citizenship rights in England was to introduce a phase of repression which lasted nearly twenty years (see Cole and Postgate 1946: 150–68). Moore (1969: 31) goes so far as to say that if the Battle of Waterloo had not removed the 'menace' of revolution 'it is highly unlikely that England would have resumed in the nineteenth century those slow and halting steps toward political and social reform that she had given up at the end of the eighteenth'.

The paramount importance of their security to ruling classes means, however, that unnerving foreign regimes and developments do not necessarily lead to domestic repression. Security may be achieved by removing the temptation of a foreign revolutionary example by offering democratic reforms to subordinate classes and dissident forces at home. In an insightful polemic on British history and politics Leon Trotsky (1925: 46–7) argues that the fear of European revolution led the English capitalist class to accept the legalization of trade unions, the extension of the suffrage, and the introduction of social reforms. These developents had been possible, according to Trotsky (1925: 36), 'so long as the English bourgeoisie, owing to its world leadership, still had in its hands great resources for its manoeuvers'. Trotsky's observations suggest that economic prosperity and foreign revolution, for instance, have quite different consequences for the development of democratic citizenship when they appear together than when they do not.

The discussion here has shown that struggle is important in the advancement of citizenship, but significantly because it disposes the dominant class and the state to accommodation and conciliation, if it is to their advantage to be so disposed. If the extension of democratic citizenship is not in the interests of the powerful then struggle is as likely to lead to repression as to the gaining of rights; indeed, more likely. Thus the interests of the dominant class (and the state) are as important as lower-class struggle for an understanding of the rise and extension of modern citizenship. In a sense Giddens (1982: 171), for instance, acknowledges the need to qualify his proposition that citizenship rights have been achieved only through struggle when he goes on to note that:

> It is surely not accidental that, in various European countries, the universal franchise was only achieved in the shadow of the First World War . . . The war helped to break down some traditional sources of resistance to social change. But governments also needed the commitment of the population to national objectives; the new citizens became cannon fodder on the battlefields of Europe.
>
> (Giddens 1982: 171–2)

Yet Giddens fails to recognize how seriously his general position is compromised when he accepts that government expedience and not only class struggle can extend citizenship rights.

Turner's qualifications of the idea that citizenship is attained through struggle are of quite a different order. Without disclaiming the significance of struggle and conflict, indeed social violence, as a precipitant of developments in democratic citizenship, he wishes to change the emphasis away from class antagonism. Turner (1986: 67) argues that while class formation and relations have been crucial to an understanding of modern capitalism as an outcome of the demise of feudalism, a number of modern societies have no feudal history and have instead developed through colonial settlement and migration. According to Turner (1986: 67) the preoccupation with class has led 'to the neglect of other components of modern social change such as war and migration' which are also crucial determinants of modern citizenship.

iii

The idea that warfare promotes citizenship, which has come to be widely accepted, is based on at least three propositions. In order to wage war states require the commitment of their populations, and this can be bought with an extension of citizenship. Secondly, warfare promotes social change through mass mobilization and state intervention; and under these conditions there emerges a new appreciation of collective and shared responsibility and the means are created whereby meaningful participation in the national community can be achieved through the expansion of citizenship, especially social citizenship. That is, in wartime people come to realize that if the dangers a country faces are to be shared, then its resources should also be shared. Finally, warfare promotes full employment and tight labour markets. Under these circumstances labour struggles are likely to put great pressure on employers and government and lead to gains for labour, including an expansion of citizenship rights.

There is another aspect to the relationship between warfare and citizenship, which has nothing to do with the matters mentioned above and is seldom treated in the literature. Yet it is a relationship which is more direct than any of those indicated in the previous paragraph. In his discussion of democratizing influences and processes in seventeen OECD countries Göran Therborn (1977: 21) refers to 'the war democracies proper', that is, countries in which modern democratic citizenship was instituted as a consequence of military defeat. Democracies by defeat include Austria, Finland, Germany, Italy, Japan and Sweden. Therborn (1977: 23) is not suggesting that this is the only war-led route to modern citizenship, for he goes on to say that wartime national mobilization has also been an important factor in the development of democratic citizenship, but largely in accelerating processes already under way. But in none of the cases that he considered was it possible to say that it was a necessary condition of an expansion of citizenship. In fact the suggestion that warfare can be held responsible for the extension of citizenship is seriously overdrawn, as we shall see, except in the case of democracies by defeat.

Historically there have been few wars which could arguably lead

to an extension of citizenship through the need to recruit a
population to patriotic objectives and through a consolidation of
resistance to pre-war privilege. Such cases typically involve universal military conscription, extensive state control over economic
organization and labour allocation, and a general societal mobilization for the war effort. Only the two World Wars, of 1914–18 and
1939–45, satisfy such requirements. Other wars have created
citizenship rights for large categories of the populations of com-
batant nations, especially revolutionary and civil wars, but few
could have done so as a consequence of social and political
processes set in motion as a secondary effect of societal war
mobilization.

Duncan Gallie (1983: 225–7) has shown that during the First
World War, in all major belligerent countries, societal war mobilization is likely to have contributed to the working-class radicalism
which at the end of the war sought a society more egalitarian than it
had been before and during hostilities. But unlike Turner (1986:
69–70) Gallie does not draw general conclusions from these
findings, for the war-promoted demands for extensions of democratic citizenship, among other things, were not met in significant
cases. Gallie's comparison of the different situations of Britain and
France is highly instructive for an understanding of the role of the
war in the development of citizenship. There is no opportunity to go
into Gallie's evidence and argument here, but some key points can
be mentioned.

Gallie (1983: 237) notes that while the governments of France
and Britain shared the same objectives in the immediate post-war
period, namely the preservation of the structure of capitalist society
in the face of a fear of impending revolution, they adopted 'very
different strategies towards their respective labour movements'.
The French government of the day, according to Gallie (1983: 242–
4), had no programme of social reform, and not only excluded the
labour movement from national political life but by 1920 had also
facilitated the destruction of its influence in industry. The British
government, on the other hand, brought in legislation which
extended the political and social citizenship of the working class
(Gallie 1983: 240).

The measures introduced by the British government after the war
were partly in return for promises made during the war by the trade
union movement and the Labour Party for support of the war-
effort. Why the British government felt that it should so commit

itself when the French government was subject to no such compulsion is to be found in the strength of the British labour movement prior to and during the war and in the weakness of the French labour movement during the same periods. Gallie (1983: 247) argues that 'a critical factor that appears to have weighed heavily on the British government's preferences for an accommodative strategy was its assessment of the potential disruptive power of organized labour in a war situation'. No similar threat faced the French government. This conclusion strongly suggests that it is misleading for Giddens (1982: 171–2) and Turner (1986: 69) to regard the attainment of citizenship through war mobilization as an alternative to its achievement through class struggle. Gallie's discussion shows that the level of class conflict is crucial to the context in which the state may need to manipulate popular commitment by the extension of citizenship rights.

But to leave the matter in these terms is unnecessarily question begging, for it suggests that warfare, together with class struggle does expand citizenship. Yet warfare, above all else, has generally diminished the rights, including the citizenship rights, exercised in pre-war times by the populations of belligerent nations. The requirements of organization for war, including the mobilization of personnel (through military conscription and civilian work-force planning), of information (through propaganda and censorship), and of *matériel* (through industrial and economic planning), all encroach on civil, political, industrial and social rights. A return to normalization in the post-war period may involve an expansion of citizenship rights relative to wartime limitations on the rights of citizens, but this hardly amounts to a causal influence of warfare on the development of citizenship. Pat Thane (1978: 18) argues that an element in the development of social citizenship following the First and Second World Wars was to 'retrieve the losses in health-care, housing and education which occurred during the war'. In those countries in which post-war expansions in citizenship rights were real (apart from Therborn's democracies by defeat) the war interrupted developments which were already under way. In Britain, for example, the foundation of industrial and social rights was firmly established in legislation passed during the period from 1906 to 1911, including the Workmens Compensation Act of 1906, the Old Age Pensions Act of 1908 and the National Insurance Act of 1911. The expansion of citizenship rights through such post-war legislation as the Representation of the People Act of 1918 and the Unemployment Insurance Act of 1920 can be more readily explained by the processes which led up to the earlier developments than by the war which came between them.

What about the third proposition of the idea that war promotes citizenship, mentioned at the beginning of this section? It is true that war creates labour shortages and that tight labour markets give workers an advantage in collective bargaining. Labour's gains under these circumstances may go beyond increases in pay and improvements in conditions and include an expansion of rights, especially of industrial citizenship. These possibilities have materialized in certain cases and in particular have been very important for the American labour-movement, which historically has enjoyed only the most limited industrial rights. It must be added that the gains American labour achieved during both World Wars were lost within two or three years of a return to post-war normalcy. This fact may be used to indicate the causal significance of war, but in the context its temporary effect cannot be used in favour of the notion. Here again war does not replace class struggle as an influence on the development of citizenship, but is simply a factor which affects a set of conditions, the shortage of labour in particular, which may enhance the bargaining power of workers. This is a very inadequate ground from which to argue that warfare expands citizenship.

It will be clear from the brief discussion here that war relates to citizenship in a number of quite different ways. First, the actual waging of war requires a diminution of citizenship rights. Second, democracy may be imposed on countries militarily defeated in war. This is not a necessary consequence of defeat, of course, but has been the cause of democratic citizenship in some significant cases. Third, the argument that war creates citizenship through social processes it sets in motion has been advanced by constructing the most 'precarious generalizations . . . on slender evidence' (Thane 1978: 18; see also Milward 1984). At best the proposition applies to wars in which societal mobilization has occurred, but certainly not to all nations subject to such mobilization. Any expansion of citizenship through war mobilization cannot be regarded as an alternative to its achievement through class struggle, and the introduction of a context of the pre-war situation tends to enormously reduce the importance of warfare to post-war developments of citizenship.

iv

In addition to war Turner (1986: 67) holds that migration, and also egalitarian ideologies, are responsible for modern democratic citizenship. Turner (1986: 71) identifies two quite distinct roles for migration in the development of citizenship. First, migration out of traditional rural cultures promotes a secularization which in turn supports the struggle for citizenship rights; and second, modern citizenship in British dominion societies, including America, has to be understood in terms of the migrant nature of those societies. The significance of a migrant basis in the development of democratic citizenship in America, Australia, Canada and New Zealand, for example, is not explicitly indicated by Turner. Any consideration of the historical development of such societies will in fact point to the importance of class relations in the rise of democratic citizenship in migrant societies.

Colonies of white settlement in which the original population was either sparse at the outset or largely eliminated during colonization are likely to share two further features: first, a chronic shortage of labour and second, a significant capitalist farming sector. The high wage structure created by the first of these reinforces the high technology and productivity of the second. The resulting class structure, free of a cash-cropping peasantry and a 'native' under-class, makes the capture of the colonial state by the settler population politically feasible. It is important to stress that it is not migration so much as the class formation of the migrant society which leads to democratic citizenship in dominion societies. Other colonies of white settlement, especially those which typically contain mining and plantation sectors drawing upon cheap indigenous labour and a peasant subsistence sector, such as Kenya and Rhodesia, have been much less successful in the development of democratic citizenship. In these cases the dominant colonial class maintains links with and indeed could be seen as a direct extension of the dominant class of the colonizing power. The settler population under these general circumstances is not able to wrest control of the state from colonial rule, and in its relations with the indigenous labour-force and peasantry has little interest in a struggle for democratic citizenship. On the contrary.

Even where a positive association of migration and citizenship might be established for the foundation of democracy, such as in the United States of America, it is misleading to assume that migration will continue to play a positive role in the development of democratic citizenship without regard to the class context in which it operates. It is generally accepted, for instance, that migration in America weakened the working-class struggle for union organization against belligerent employers and a hostile state, and therefore significantly retarded the development of industrial citizenship. Also, the fragmentary, indeed divisive composition of the American working class, sponsored by European immigration and American rural emmigration to the cities, contributed to the shrinking of civil rights from about the 1890s and certainly after 1918. There is nothing intrinsic to migration which leads it to support the growth of democratic citizenship. Its significance seems to be in its contribution to class forces and relationships, and it may have a negative and not only a positive effect on the development of citizenship.

The role of emmigration from traditional cultures in the process of secularization, mentioned by Turner in the context of the rise of modern citizenship, is analogous to the role of warfare in breaking down traditionalism through the involvement of women, for example, in war production. Both of these may be related to the rise of citizenship, but only indirectly. They serve as possible background factors, along with egalitarian ideology, mentioned by Turner (1986: 73) as a further condition for the emergence of modern citizenship. Egalitarian, universalistic and, presumably, secular ideologies, Turner (1986: 74) says, are important resources of social groups in conflict with given social arrangements and struggling for modern citizenship.

There is no doubt that 'modernizing' ideologies encourage those struggling for rights and conditions denied by an existing organization of society. Yet the ideologies Turner refers to are just as likely to arise out of the struggle for democratic citizenship as to be its cause. Of course the relationship will inevitably become reciprocal and contextual; but this simply suggests that the proposition that ideology is a 'resource' in the struggle for citizenship is misleading, and, as Barrington Moore (1969: 486) says, 'circular'. This is not to say that ideology has no function in the rise of modern citizenship. But it is likely that the demise of old ideologies may be more important than the rise of new ones in the direct struggle for citizenship rights. In particular, the collapse of classical political economy in early nineteenth-century England, as a doctrine or ideology of capitalist class organization which sustained opposition to the 'combination' of labour, among other things, was probably more directly significant in the struggle for political, industrial and social rights than any other single cultural or ideological factor (see Clarke 1982: 128–36).

v

The rise of modern democratic citizenship has occurred in a number of different historical, societal and institutional contexts. The significance of capitalist development and especially the capitalist class structure for the expansion of citizenship is not confined to those societies which arose out of the collapse of feudalism, but extends to all societies in which democratic citizenship has a real presence. The attainment of citizenship through struggle, and especially class struggle, reflects not only the impact of lower-class demands but also dominant class requirements for security. In this chapter it has been argued that the rise, development and expansion of citizenship rights reflects the changing capacities and needs of class forces in capitalist society.

4

Citizenship and Class Inequality

Historically power has been both concentrated and unitary. Political and economic powers, for instance, could be functionally differentiated only as distinct aspects of a single power. In practically all of its instances the human experience has shown that those who possess economic power also control government and law. It is arguably this situation which has provoked and is challenged by the rise of democratic citizenship. The struggle for citizenship has been the struggle against exclusion, and against the inequalities which exclusion produces. But the rise of democratic citizenship has not brought an end to inequality. Rather it has produced spheres of equal participation which parallel those of exclusive power.

The above remarks are unquestionably applicable to a citizenship comprised of civil and political rights. The development of civil citizenship introduced not only equality before the law but also law as an institution free of and formally separate from private property. Indeed, the removal of legal privilege through citizenship was at the same time the separation of legal institutions from economic power. The advent of political citizenship similarly provided for political equality by taking government, or the means of selecting the individuals from which a government could be formed, away from the exclusive control of economic-power holders. Thus the advance of citizenship has meant the displacement of exclusion with universal participation, but only in those elements of the erstwhile unitary configuration of power which have been separated from its economic core. It is thus important to remember that while citizenship rights are universal, the principle of citizenship has never been generalized to all social institutions. The economic system in particular and the social classes associated with it remain exclusive in nature and marked by a high degree of inequality and concentration of power. It is on these bases that the capitalist class system can be contrasted with the system of democratic citizenship.

It is pertinent to ask whether social citizenship, which directly addresses the problem of economic inequality, has been more successful against economic exclusion than civil and political citizenship.

i

There can be no doubt that the development of citizenship during the twentieth century has altered the pattern of social inequality. Yet it would be unnecessarily narrow to suggest that citizenship was the only factor in this process. Improvements in the conditions of ordinary people can in many instances be attributed to directly economic causes. The consolidation of the world economy by the 1890s and the international economic competition which accompanied it led employers to improve the conditions of employment for most of their workers in order to raise labour productivity. In addition, new technologies not only destroyed the lowest-paid jobs, and therefore raised the wage floor of inequality, but also formed part of a new situation which enhanced the bargaining power of organized labour. The prosperity of the period from the late 1940s, which (until recently) has been responsible for the most optimistic outlooks on the decline of inequality, is also most readily explained in economic terms. Full employment, expanding mass markets and the development of new technologies and their application to production led to rises in living standards which appeared to further reduce the inequalities which had more or less been declining since the turn of the century.

It is to his credit that Marshall (1950: 96) recognizes that while the first advances in social rights from the end of the nineteenth century were to make inroads on the pattern of inequality, other forces were at work as well. But the reduction of inequality through economic causes and through citizenship are not unconnected for Marshall. He says that the 'diminution of inequality strengthened the demand for its abolition' and goes on to add that such aspirations have partly been achieved by 'incorporating social rights in the status of citizenship and thus creating a universal right to real income which is not proportionate to the market value of the claimant' (Marshall 1950: 96). Thus Marshall draws citizenship back into the argument in which the decline of inequality can be shown to have a basis in economic developments.

It is in fact crucial to recognize that non-economic sources have influenced the structure of inequality. This is not only to more adequately account for those changes themselves, but also in order to understand the significance of such changes for more general political and social developments. The question immediately arises whether the provision of economic resources as a right of citizenship alters not only the pattern of inequality but its very basis, and therefore the dynamic and structure of class society.

One possibility is that rights to social goods and services might simply improve the conditions of the disadvantaged without directly dealing with the underlying causes of inequality. Such changes may mitigate the harm economic inequalities cause to individuals by slinging a safety-net of social policy under the disadvantaged. If this is the general outcome of social citizenship, then the principles underlying the operations of the economy and the structure and process of social class remain untouched by its development. It is possible that under such circumstances social tensions will be reduced and that class antagonism will decline. These things tend not to affect the actual structure of class inequality, however, but serve to legitimate it and therefore preserve class privilege and advantage. Under these circumstances the effect of citizenship on the system of class inequality is primarily political and apologetic.

A quite different possibility is that social citizenship, and therefore the provision of economic resources as a right, may modify the very principle of economic relationships. Certainly the non-market provision of economic resources would have been inconceivable to the *laissez-faire* capitalism of the nineteenth century. According to its principles workers separated from the means of material production are compelled to sell their capacity to labour for a wage in order to live. Those unable to derive a livelihood from the labour market in this way had no other access to means of subsistence (except as a dependent wife or child of those in employment). This harsh and direct relationship between the labour market and income has been modified by social citizenship. It is thus possible to argue that the structure of modern society is subject to a different basis of development than the one which governed *laissez-faire* capitalism, and therefore that market in-equalities no longer determine social differentiation. Bryan Turner (1986: 6), who accepts this view, summarizes it by saying that 'citizenship is an abatement of the class structure of capitalist economic relationships'.

Marshall's analysis in *Citizenship and Social Class* is not clearly directed to either of the positions mentioned here, although his arguments are most readily associated with the second of them. It is important to recognize, however, just how tenuous and inconclusive are Marshall's views. Too many readers have ignored the conjectural tone of Marshall's (1950: 115) statement that 'it may be that the inequalities permitted, and even moulded by citizenship do not any longer constitute class distinctions in the sense in which that term is used for past societies'. Those same readers will have missed the fact that Marshall immediately says that such a question cannot be answered, for 'our ignorance on this matter is profound'. What he does insist upon is that 'the preservation of economic inequalities has been made more difficult by the enrichment of the status of citizenship' and also that there 'are limits inherent in the egalitarian movement' (Marshall 1950: 117). Marshall's (1950: 117) conclusion that 'class distinctions may survive which have no appropriate economic function, and economic differences which do not correspond with accepted class distinctions' seriously requires interpretation.

In order to assess the impact of the development of citizenship on class inequality it is necessary to identify the changes in the pattern of inequality which are attributable to citizenship rights. When this is done it can be asked in what way such changes affect the nature and operation of the capitalist class system.

ii

The relationship between the expansion of citizenship, especially through the realization of social citizenship, and social and economic inequalities is complex. In principle social citizenship has the effect of encouraging equality of opportunity and is therefore entirely compatible with certain inequalities of condition or outcome. Thus not only might social citizenship reduce some inequalities, but by promoting achievement by merit it may create new ones. Marshall is quite explicit on this point. He says, for example, that the right of the citizen in social selection and mobility is the right to equality of educational opportunity, which has the aim of eliminating hereditary privilege. The establishment of such a system will initially reveal what Marshall (1950: 109) calls 'hidden equalities' for it will permit poor children to show that they are as bright and capable as rich children. 'But the final outcome', he continues, 'is a structure of unequal status fairly apportioned to unequal abilities'. This conclusion is crucial for it demonstrates, as Marshall (1950: 110) acknowledges, that 'citizenship operates as an instrument of social stratification'.

The character of the inequalities created by the practice of citizenship rights is that they are legitimate: 'The status acquired by education is carried out into the world bearing the stamp of legitimacy, because it has been conferred by an institution designed to give the citizen his just rights' (Marshall 1950: 110). Elsewhere in *Citizenship and Social Class* Marshall (1950: 70) says that the assumption that the basic equality of citizenship rights is consistent with the inequalities of social class is demonstrated in the fact that 'citizenship has itself become, in certain respects, the architect of legitimate social inequality'. Citizenship is thus not opposed to inequality as such but to illegitimate inequality, to inequality which cannot be justified on a basis of equal citizenship rights (Marshall 1950: 117).

In his discussion of the modern class system, in which class differences 'emerge from the interplay of a variety of factors related to the institutions of property and education and the structure of the national economy', Marshall (1950: 85) notes that in such a system social inequality 'provides the incentive to effort and designs the distribution of power'. A feature of such an arrangement, however, is that as the general pattern of inequality does not correspond to an *a priori* value system which designates the appropriate range of inequality for each level, inequality 'though necessary, may become excessive' (Marshall 1950: 85–6). Thus necessary inequality must be distinguished from excessive inequality, from poverty or destitution. Both are part of the capitalist class system; the latter is definitely incompatible with social citizenship and so is the former if it is not legitimate. The basis on which legitimate inequality is *necessary* under conditions of universal social rights is not clear, for while Marshall (1950: 100) says that under these conditions there is a 'need to preserve differential incomes as a source of economic incentive' he also insists that work ceases to be a market need and becomes instead a duty (Marshall 1950: 117–8). The principle remains, nevertheless, and Marshall (1972: 117) repeats it in a later paper, 'Value Problems of Welfare-Capitalism', when he says that in modern democratic society 'poverty is a disease, but inequality is an essential structural feature'.

Relief of destitution pre-dates social citizenship, of course. Nineteenth-century philanthropy and charity attacked the excesses of the class system, but they failed to question its principles (Marshall 1950: 86). The incorporation of social rights in the status of citizenship, on the other hand, not only affects destitution and therefore raises the social minimum, but according to Marshall (1950: 96) it 'has assumed the guise of action modifying the whole pattern of social inequality'. In removing poverty but not necessarily legitimate inequality by the means of rights universally available to all citizens (and not simply the impoverished) not only has the base-line of inequality been raised but the entire structure of inequality has been changed. It is not our purpose to ask whether the enrichment of citizenship has in fact eradicated poverty (a number of studies have shown that throughout the period corresponding with the rise of social citizenship in Britain significant pockets of destitution remained) but to consider how the system of social class might be altered by the development of citizenship.

It is only through the incorporation of social rights that citizenship could bring about any direct change to the pattern of social inequality. The legal powers given by civil rights were entirely limited by the fact that their use was 'drastically curtailed by class prejudice and lack of economic opportunity', as Marshall (1950: 95) put it. Political rights had a greater potential for modifying the structure of inequality, but as they required 'experience, organization and a change of ideas as to the proper functions of government', all which take time to develop, their direct impact has been less than impressive (Marshall 1950: 95). Industrial citizenship more clearly addresses the problem of inequality, but as it functions through the institutions of the labour market, collective bargaining tends to 'standardize' rather than challenge wage stratification (Marshall 1950: 113). It is for this reason that Marshall (1972: 118) is later able to say that collective bargaining gives formal recognition to differentials which already exist, so that in a democracy trade unions help to legitimize inequalities rather than abolish them.

Social rights are able to affect the pattern of inequality directly because they permit the provision of benefits in kind which may lead the real income of a citizen to be much greater than their money income. The importance of inequalities formed through market exchanges is seriously reduced when economic values become available outside the market as a universal right of citizenship. This is especially so when these benefits are not only transfer payments but services and resources provided without the intervention of a market exchange but through the state administration of social services. Such developments modify the pattern of inequality directly by reconstituting the distribution of real income and also by altering the significance of the inequalities which remain.

Marshall (1950: 102) says that the 'extension of the social services is not primarily a means of equalizing incomes'. He regards this as unimportant. What really matters, he says, 'is that there is a general enrichment of the concrete substance of civilized life, a general reduction of risk and insecurity, an equalization between the more and the less fortunate at all levels'. Marshall (1950: 102–3) goes on to argue that

> Equalization is not so much between classes as between individuals within a population which is now treated for this purpose as though it were one class. Equality of status is more important than equality of income.

Before considering what 'equalization' and 'equality of status' mean here it is important to recognize that while equalization of income cannot be an outcome of social rights the distributional changes Marshall envisages are nonetheless quite significant.

The universal right to social services does not merely lift the base-line from which legitimate inequality begins, but raises the guaranteed minimum to a level which renders 'the term "minimum" . . . a misnomer', according to Marshall (1950: 104). His reference here is to a desired or intentional state rather than to the actual practice of social citizenship as it had developed at the time of his writing, or since for that matter. But it is clear that Marshall believes that under conditions of social citizenship the 'provided service, not the purchased service, becomes the norm of social welfare'. The significance of this is that there is a tendency for the advantages derived from having a larger money income to be confined to an increasingly more limited or narrower area of consumption the more social citizenship is enhanced by the expansion of the social services (Marshall 1950: 120). It is precisely his conjecture of this tendency which encourages Marshall (1950: 119) to argue that the incorporation of social rights in citizenship leads social inequalities to become 'economically functionless', so that only those 'class distinctions may survive which have no appropriate economic function' (Marshall 1950: 117).

It is not simply through the progressive divergence of real and money incomes that social citizenship modifies class, but also in a 'class fusion' which Marshall (1950: 103) says is 'expressed in the form of a new common experience'. While earlier forms of class-abatement alleviated the condition of poverty they tended to reinforce the class divisions between those to whom the services were provided and those who did not require them. The universalization of social services as a right of citizenship, on the other hand, has meant that the vast majority of citizens are subject to the same process through which the services are provided and receive essentially the same benefit. This common experience reduces the social distance between citizens. 'The extension of such services', Marshall (1950: 103) says, 'can therefore have a profound effect on the qualitative aspects of social differentiation'. In this sense, then, class distinctions which separate persons are reduced, and their significance diminished. Here is the 'equality of status' which Marshall was quoted above as saying is 'more important than equality of income'. This is because it is a qualitative equalization between persons which reduces the social importance of class distinctions.

The argument that citizenship modifies social class does not assume the equalization of income but holds, rather, that through social rights the base-line of inequality is raised and the remaining inequalities tend to become economically functionless and socially legitimate. Thus hierarchy remains, but is of a quite different consequence than it is under conditions of market determination. Marshall (1950: 120) does not deny that differences in money incomes can provide real advantages to those with higher earnings, but adds that the trend towards equalization of real incomes through social citizenship has the effect of giving wage differentials an importantly symbolic significance, so that they operate as 'labels attached to industrial status, not only as instruments of genuine economic stratification'. Marshall's point here is that manual workers, for instance, may accept as proper the disparity between their earnings and those of certain grades of clerical workers, provided that they have 'the same general amenities as are enjoyed by salaried employees'. The rationale which Marshall (1950: 120) advances for this position is that if all workers enjoy the same amenities, 'reflect[ing] the fundamental equality of all citizens and not the inequalities of earnings or occupational grades', then these latter inequalities will not be contentious. Here citizenship functions to reduce class resentment.

Again, there is no need to assess the empirical accuracy of Marshall's argument. It is presented tentatively and stated as a tendency or trend rather than as an accomplished fact. Also Marshall (1950: 121) acknowledges that not all classes accept the pattern of inequality emergent through social citizenship. There is no need to doubt that Marshall accurately records the satisfaction of manual workers with social benefits, but it would be much more difficult to demonstrate the normative acceptance of the unequal wage structure which he projects. People tend to support arrangements which benefit them and to question those which are to their disadvantage. If there continues to be a real advantage in higher earnings those with lower incomes will have grounds for dissatisfaction. The important point for the discussion here is that Marshall postulates a relationship between social citizenship and class resentment which holds that as the one develops the other will decline.

iii

Social citizenship removes the economic function from inequality and class distinctions by the means of a 'progressive divorce between real and money incomes', as Marshall (1950: 119) puts it. Such developments have indeed altered the complexion of class relations in removing labour from what Max Weber (1925: 277) describes as the 'compulsion of the whip of hunger', which he saw as a requirement for the existence of modern capitalism. Through the provision of social security, and therefore a real income not based wholly on the recipient's market situation, workers no longer face the choice of employment or starvation, for unemployment no longer means destitution. In this sense citizenship has tempered the power of capitalists in particular and employers in general in their dealings with workers. But it would be difficult to go on from here to argue that social rights have rendered class distinctions economically functionless. Social security has been important in reducing the risks associated with unemployment, for instance, by providing an alternative (if incomplete) source of means of subsistence. But the area of personal consumption cannot be the full locus of class experience any more than it can be the entire substance of economic inequality, as Marshall's argument implies.

Income inequality is not unimportant, of course; but it does not cover the whole pattern of inequality associated with 'economic functions' and class differences. While Marshall (1950: 88–90) mentions that during the eighteenth and nineteenth centuries wealth interfered with the exercise of equality before the law and political rights, he wholly downplays the continuing role of wealth in economic inequality. Inequalities of wealth remain in many ways more important than income inequalities for an understanding of the characteristics and dynamics of social stratification and class. The ownership of physical and financial assets provides opportunities and powers which are far more extensive than those offered by the receipt of a wage or salary. Although potentially subject to legislative intervention property ownership is not directly modified by social citizenship.

Persons who possess property (including the family house) enjoy a number of advantages over those who do not. Perhaps the most pervasive economic function of wealth is its role in borrowing money. As funds are generally loaned against existing assets wealth permits property owners to spend in excess of their current income. This means that the tendency for social citizenship to narrow the range of the distribution of real income is counteracted by the borrowing capacity of the wealthy, which widens it. Inequalities of wealth are not rendered economically functionless by the incorporation of social rights in citizenship. On the contrary, wealth continues to be the principal determinant of economic well-being in spite of the provision of benefits which might increase the real income of social citizens.

Because the possession of personal property varies by degree through the population the general significance of wealth is in its effect on the structure of stratification, not class. The possible grades or levels of inequalities of wealth are numerous and the differences between contiguous grades are not necessarily large even though the distance between the bottom and the top levels may be vast. In treating wealth it is therefore necessary to distinguish between property as a right of personal possession and property as capital, for only the latter relates to clear differences of a class nature (Parkin 1979: 48–52). Private ownership as capital in the means of production provides an economic function to class distinctions which is totally untouched by the development of citizenship.

In capitalist society direct access to private property in the means of production entails control over the circumstances in which others are implicated and therefore implies a direct social power. As Andrew Hacker (1965: 139–44) and Charles Lindblom

(1977: 171–5), for example, have shown, the technical, industrial and market structures of whole societies are determined by capital investment. Thus in exercising the power of private property one class has power over others in determining the nature and availability of jobs, the economic security of those employed in them, and the quality and prices of the means of life. Here is an economic function which remains unaffected by the progressive divorce between real and money incomes and which continues to characterize class differences and class relations after the full development of modern democratic citizenship.

It will be clear that the augmentation of real income through the provision of universal social rights could remove the economic function of inequality only in certain areas of personal consumption. The economic functions of personal wealth and private capital are untouched by these developments and their significance for the total pattern of class inequality remains unchanged. That part of Marshall's argument which holds that social citizenship modifies class inequality is therefore unsubstantiated. As Ralf Dahrendorf (1959: 107) indicates, Marshall's account of the levelling effect of social citizenship is 'ultimately simply irrelevant for the problem of class' as it deals with an entirely different subject, namely that of social stratification. It has been shown here that even as a treatment of stratification Marshall's account is in fact incomplete as it ignores the economic function of wealth or personal property.

The idea that citizenship modifies social class is more directly suggested in Marshall's treatment of the effect of social rights on the qualitative as opposed to the quantitative aspects of social differentiation. In particular Marshall (1950: 103) argues that the universalization of social services is the basis of a common experience which promotes 'class fusion'. It is notable that none of those who have commented on Marshall's arguments or based their own on his have considered Marshall's conceptualization of social class; it has simply been taken for granted. But it is only when it is clear what is meant by 'class' that we can know whether social rights might promote 'class fusion', for instance. It is not possible in the present discussion to adequately treat the concept of class in Marshall, but it is necessary to outline what he understands by the term.

A theme which runs through much of Marshall's writing is that social class exists by virtue of the social perceptions and relations internal to it. While Marshall acknowledges that economic forces underwrite social classes he insists that by themselves they generate differences between economic levels rather than class differences. The latter are based on an awareness persons have of experiences they share or fail to share with others. Thus in Marshall's view social class is ultimately a culturally constructed phenomenon. In an early essay Marshall (1934: 110) says that 'social classes are identity groups existing for the sake of the internal contacts which identity makes possible' and that class differences are 'defined by an attitude of comparison which recognizes qualitative differences'. While Marshall (1973: xxii) excluded the essay containing these quotations from his later collection of sociological papers because he felt that it was 'not only "preliminary" but naive, and so out of date . . . that it was more likely to confuse than to enlighten', the general conception of class expressed in it continues to appear in his subsequent work.

In *Citizenship and Social Class*, for instance, Marshall (1950: 110) restates the idea that social class consists in an awareness of what people believe they have in common:

> Differences within each class are ignored as irrelevant; differences between classes are given exaggerated significance. Thus qualities which are in reality strung out along a continuous scale are made to create a hierarchy of groups.

Thus it is the selective social perception and interpretation of differences which leads to class inequalities, for the objective differences themselves are more or less continuous. It follows that class differences might be reduced, indeed eliminated, by altering social attitudes. It is of particular interest that in a paper which pre-dates *Citizenship and Social Class* by over a decade, but which contains a summary of its argument, Marshall proposes precisely this measure as a possible means of attaining a classless society. In 'The Nature of Class Conflict' Marshall (1938: 164–5) says that

> the institution of class teaches the members of a society to notice some differences and to ignore others when arranging persons in order of social merit. In a word, social class could not exist unless certain inequalities were regarded as irrelevant to the determination of social status. It follows that there are two main roads to the classless society. One leads through the abolition (as far as possible) of the social differences between individuals – which is roughly the way of communism – and the other proceeds by rendering all differences irrelevant to social status – which is roughly the way of democracy.

It is now possible to appreciate the grounds on which Marshall argues that the common experience of social security as a universal right of citizenship leads to 'class fusion'. Marshall believes that such an experience will promote an awareness of a common situation among citizens which will tend to over-ride or at least reduce the relevance and social visibility of differences between them. As Marshall (1953: 254) later acknowledges, this situation will tend to reduce social class differences only in so far as it reduces distinctive class cultures, while economic inequalities may remain.

The identity of class divisions with social perceptual or cultural differences, which is explicit in Marshall's conception of class, indicates a seriously inadequate treatment of the problem. Class contains a cultural element, certainly. But social classes cannot exist as discrete entities; and social class cannot be defined by the conception held by its members of their relations with others. Any difference between the cultures of different classes will largely derive from the asymmetrical relations between classes *qua* classes. That classes are superordinate or subordinate, dominating or subject to domination, is ultimately responsible for the different social perceptions and relations of the persons within them. Unless this fact is included in the definition we are not dealing with classes but merely with culturally defined groups. The relations between social classes are prior to the relations within them, and inter-class relations are determined by such things as the power of private property in the means of production, mentioned above, which is not 'strung out on a continuous scale' but yields a clear division between those who do and those who do not possess it.

Common experiences across the divisions of social inequality may mediate the cultural boundaries which separate social classes. Such a development will not reduce the distance between classes, although it may permit individuals to feel that the differences between them which remain should be regarded as less important than what they have come to share through the development of a common social citizenship. These things do not indicate a 'class fusion' as Marshall supposes, for the bases of class differences in the relations of domination and subordination are untouched by the harmonizing social perceptions which he hypothesizes will emerge with social citizenship. Indeed, the changes in the 'qualitative aspects of social differentiation' which Marshall describes as resulting from the universalization of social services will be highly unstable if the class relations he ignores remain unchanged. The equalization of persons as citizens might affect the social perception of social differences but it cannot modify the material relations between the classes. In other words the development of citizenship rights may change the way in which people identify themselves and it may alter their feelings about social and class inequalities. But that is all.

This last point is amplified in a paper which clarifies and corrects a number of the ambiguities of *Citizenship and Social Class*. In 'Changes in Social Stratification in the Twentieth Century' Marshall (1956: 130) sets out to answer the question 'Has class . . . been losing importance as a feature of social structure?' He says that it would 'be rash to conclude that class has been losing its importance; but it may be true that it has been changing its character' (Marshall 1956: 138). The change in character referred to here is a supposition that the inequalities between classes are becoming not much greater than those within them. The important point for our purposes is not Marshall's assessment of the pattern of stratification, but his insistence that these developments do not undermine the class system but alter only class identity and class resentment. For instance, Marshall (1956: 131) notes that ethnic and religious affiliations – today one might add sexual identity – have tended to displace class loyalty 'as a determinant of social action'. Also, Marshall (1956: 137) indicates that rising levels of consumption, developments of citizenship rights, and structural changes in the economy which make 'the distribution of property less decisively determinant of the distribution of power' have tended to lessen the resentment felt between members of different classes. Class resentment influences the propensity for conflict while class loyalty influences the self-identity of those engaged in conflict, or some other form of group involvement or membership. Declines in class resentment and in class loyalty tend to reduce and disperse class conflict. They tend to harmonize antagonistic class relations.

If the equality of citizenship status did allow manual workers, for example, to accept as proper the disparity between their earnings and those of clerical and administrative workers it would not follow that the class structure of capitalist economic relationships had been abated. If wage differentials come to have a symbolic function for workers, indicating status rather than economic stratification, they will continue to have an economic function for employers and managers, and for the share-holders

and owners of the companies they control. Class differences will not
have been eliminated even if class resentment has been reduced.

iv

Patterns of inequality or stratification may be modified by developments in citizenship rights, although it is necessary to recognize that
other forces are also at work in this process. The class structure,
however, cannot be changed by universal social rights, which treat
only distributional arrangements and ignore the institutions of
economic and social power which preserve class domination and
exploitation. Rather than alter the class structure citizenship tends
to legitimate it by contributing to a decline of class identity and
resentment. The issues associated with this suggestion will be more
fully treated in Chapter 6 below. It should be noted that the
provision of equal citizenship rights may promote an awareness of
the great inequalities of economic advantage which such rights
themselves cannot remove and therefore encourage inter-class
comparisons which promote class resentment and conflict (Bendix
1964: 101–2; Lockwood 1974: 366). Unfortunately it has not been
possible to treat this matter here. In this chapter it has been shown
that the extension of citizenship rights cannot itself alter the system
of class which operates in capitalist societies.

The argument, that while civil rights are indispensible to class
inequality, political and social rights tend to challenge it, requires
revision. Marshall (1950: 84) begins by saying that citizenship and
class are 'opposing principles'. A few pages later he suggests that
such formulations are exaggerated and that it is more appropriate to
say that citizenship has 'imposed modifications' on social class
(Marshall 1950: 110). This last phrase would be correct if it were
acknowledged that the modifications in question were extremely
modest ones, and that the basic reality of the class structure remains
unaffected by citizenship rights. Citizenship and class are based on
opposing principles, as Marshall says; one on equality and freedom,
the other on inequality and domination. But the things to which the
equality of citizenship refer are not the same as those which make
up class inequality. It is for this reason that citizenship and social
class can continue to exist together. If their co-existence is
sometimes full of tension it is not because of any logical incompatibility between them, but is rather a result of the endeavours of
socially subordinate groups to overcome their disadvantages and
lay claim to rights which may not be realized in an unequal society.

5

Social Citizenship and the Welfare State

It was shown in the previous chapter that social equality cannot be achieved through the development of citizenship and especially the social services and welfare measures. Indeed, it is Marshall's (1950: 70, 102) contention that the equality of status in citizenship makes economic and class inequality acceptable. Thus Marshall rejects the Fabian and parliamentary-socialist idea that social rights ultimately undermine capitalist principles of social organization. Marshall's view is not that social rights are victorious over the capitalist class system, but that they eliminate the class tensions implicit in market relationships, which are themselves unable to provide social and economic security to those who enter them. It is thus not necessary to demonstrate here that the welfare state has failed to redress the balance of class disadvantage (see, for example, Parkin 1971; le Grand 1982). Such arguments are less relevant to Marshall's analysis than they are to those who insist upon a parliamentary route to a classless society. This is not to say that a consideration of the welfare state from the perspective of social citizenship is without difficulty.

Three issues in particular must be considered in this context. First, it cannot be maintained that social rights and the welfare state are equivalent, although it is generally assumed that they are. Second, given that social policy is by nature directed toward particular social groups or issues, it has to be asked in what way social rights can be universal or citizenship rights. A third issue which requires elaboration is the apparent contradiction between Marshall's insistence that the principle of social citizenship is opposed to the principle of the market and his claim that social citizenship modifies but does not eliminate market capitalism. Before treating these matters it is necessary to say something about the recent origins of social policy.

i

Marshall (1950: 93–4) argues that in acceding to the union movement's demand for collective bargaining the British state in the late
nineteenth century effectively accepted the claim that workers were
entitled to certain social rights. It is not clear that this account
emphasizes the positive role of the state at the expense of
working-class action, as Giddens (1982: 172), for instance, suggests.
It is true, however, that Marshall does fail to elaborate the idea that
social or welfare rights were won by the working class in struggle.
The proposition that the welfare state is a consequence of the
growing strength of the labour movement and its struggle to
transform capitalism has in recent years attained some prominence
(Castles 1978; Korpi 1978; Stephens 1979). That Marshall avoids
the suggestion that the state provision of social security can be
understood as a victory of working-class demands has been a focus
of criticism against him (Giddens 1982: 176; Turner 1986: 38). It is
therefore appropriate to say something about the historical argument.

Social policy redresses the condition of disadvantage, but support
for such policy need not be confined to the disadvantaged themselves. Indeed, diverse social interests may be satisfied by measures
directed to a section only of the population. Support for such
measures cannot therefore be assumed to be limited to its primary
beneficiaries. Asa Briggs (1961: 30) notes the interest of 'philanthropic businessmen wishing to improve the "efficiency" and
strengthen the "social justice" of the business system; and [of]
politicians and governments anxious to avoid what seemed to be
dangerous political consequences of unemployment'. Employers
have at times accepted that welfare measures might contribute to
economic efficiency and social control. And while it is highly
unlikely that employers would collectively support welfare legislation they have always been prepared to intervene in the formation
of welfare policy to ensure that their interests are not neglected.

While the constituency of welfare policy clearly extends beyond
its direct consumers, it has to be recognized that the direct
recipients of the benefits of social policy have not always supported
them. For instance, practically all sections of the labour movement
were concerned with the poor working conditions and low pay
which characterized British industry at the turn of the century, and
with the abject circumstances of the unemployed, but there was no
agreement that a solution lay in state-provided insurance and

benefits. Indeed, a significant section of trade union opinion during this period argued that the state's role in alleviating poverty should be confined to economic policies which supported full employment and adequate pay; social policies were regarded as means of propping up an unsatisfactory *status quo* (Thane 1978a: 95; 1982: 61–2). Of course such opinions soon ceased to have any significance. The labour movement itself changed quickly during this period as a result of the unionization of non-craft and non-skilled workers. At about the same time the activities and campaigns of philanthropic men and women, and organizations, contributed to a change in the general climate of opinion.

The indirect effect of philanthropic activity in particular had a real importance for the development of welfare legislation. The settlement house movement of the 1880s, for instance, brought educated young men into direct contact with the poor on an everyday basis. It was no accident, as Hugh Heclo (1974: 161) observes, that '[n]early all of the major architects of British social legislation during the first two decades of the twentieth century had had settlement-house experience'. The influence of philanthropy was not confined to legislators and state administrators. In spite of its name the National Committee of Organized Labour for the Promotion of Old Age Pensions, founded in 1899, was initiated and organized by non-working-class liberal reformers (Heclo 1974: 165–6). The campaign for non-contributory old-age pensions which it sponsored came to have the support of the labour movement, and was part of the process of removing working-class hostility to social legislation.

It is possible, though, to overstate or misconstrue the role of philanthropy in the creation of social legislation. Any account of the landmark National Insurance Act of 1911, for instance, would be seriously flawed if it failed to recognize not only the role of employers, who were able to influence the process of amendment to secure their interests (Hay 1978: 119), but also the crucial role of medical practitioners. The 1911 Act, among other things, provided working-class breadwinners with medical benefits and a free choice of doctor. Prior to the passage of the legislation friendly societies, trade unions and countless other institutions and groups contracted to provide medical services for their members. Within this system doctors were wholly dependent on voluntary associations and private enterprises for their work and their professional values. The National Insurance Act has been described as the culmination of a struggle by doctors to free themselves from the contract system which exercised almost complete power over them (Titmuss 1959: 306–8). The general point here is that social policy requires an administrative and professional infrastructure which has its own interests in the formation and direction of state activity.

Welfare legislation also serves the direct interests of government. Social security legislation was pioneered not by labour movements or social-democratic regimes but by Bismarck's compulsory insurance laws of 1882, 1884 and 1889, which protected German workers against the effects of sickness, accident, old age and invalidity. The founding legislation of British social security, the Old Age Pensions Act of 1908 and the National Insurance Act of 1911, was put in place by the Asquith Liberal Government. It is of interest that this legislation passed through the House of Lords unscathed by the Conservative opposition, and that the previous Conservative administration had itself passed the Unemployed Workmens Act of 1905. The support by governments for social security legislation comes from two related concerns. Such legislation may be perceived as a basis of electoral success, and it may be conceived as a means to social and political stability.

The extension of the suffrage in England through the Second Reform Bill of 1867 created the conditions for both the Conservative and the Liberal Parties to attempt to attract the vote of the newly enfranchised urban male workers. By the beginning of the twentieth century both parties saw policies providing social benefits and insurance as a means of electoral success. Not only did this encourage the Liberal administration to enact welfare legislation, it inhibited Conservative opposition to it. But the advent of working-class political rights not only affected the nature of the competition between parliamentary parties, it posed a potential threat to the established political and social order itself.

The extension of the franchise created a need in the British state to 'educate our masters'. The Education Act of 1870 set up elected school boards to provide schools in areas where there were no denominational schools. By 1891 elementary education was compulsory and free. Social policy has always had a similar integrative function. In addition to drawing electoral support from the working-class vote, social policy served to draw support away from emerging independent political and industrial actions of organized labour. The interest of employers and politicians in this matter increased enormously after the success of the newly formed Labour

Party in the 1906 election and the rise of industrial militancy after 1909 (Middlemas 1979: 38). A contemporary commentator drew similar conclusions for the Germany of the 1880s:

> [Bismarck's] aim in promoting industrial reforms was to cut the ground beneath the Socialistic agitators by gradually removing those grievances of which they could with only too much justice complain
>
> (Dawson 1890: 45)

More recent writers have arrived at the same conclusion (Briggs 1961: 36; Parkin 1971: 124–5). By increasing the dependence of its recipients on the state and by making dissent and agitation less attractive, social welfare can be a means of preserving or safeguarding an existing political and economic order. Social legislation does bring changes and reforms, certainly; and ordinary people benefit from these. But such legislation can serve to preserve an existing pattern of power and privilege and may leave it essentially intact.

For the reasons briefly outlined here social welfare cannot be explained directly in terms of working-class action and preference. Other interests, sometimes anti-labour interests, have been leading forces in achieving or shaping social legislation. This is not to say that working-class agitation has no place in an account of the rise of social security. From the 1880s in Britain the growth of working-class organization contributed enormously to a growing general awareness of the serious consequences of low pay and unemployment. A desire for remedies was not restricted to the working-class movement, but its growth gave urgency to the question of social reform. Such reform as was enacted satisfied interests beyond working-class needs, but the growth of labour and social movements stimulated the expansion of social welfare. It is necessary to add, as Thane (1982: 123) says, that:

> This was not simply, as is sometimes assumed, because workers demanded it, for they were often divided on the issue or actively hostile to state welfare. It derived partly from the desire of employers and politicians to check the very growth of labour.

It is therefore not possible to explain the creation of social policy simply in terms of working-class demands for state welfare and social security. Once social legislation is in place, however, its provisions become part of the structure of conditions on which working-class people in particular come to rely. When these conditions and the social security measures which are a part of them come to be threatened, as they are by governments throughout the developed capitalist world today, then it is likely that there will be struggle to defend them. Thus Giddens (1982: 176) is correct to say that the welfare state is a pivot of class conflict and not simply a means to dilute or dissolve it. But this formulation can only summarize the situation of defending existing social security arrangements which have come under threat, not that of founding welfare legislation and practices.

Marshall's failure to give central importance to working-class struggle in the formation of the welfare state can only partly indicate the limitations of his approach. There are more serious difficulties with the treatment of the welfare state in terms of social rights. Unfortunately these have been ignored in most commentaries on the limitations of Marshall's understanding of the welfare state.

ii

The identity of social rights with social policy is implicit in Marshall's treatment of the development of citizenship. This equation is historically limited, however, and logically flawed. While Marshall came to accept that social policy does not necessarily express social rights, his historical discussion in *Citizenship and Social Class* ignores an alternative understanding of 'social rights' which was used by those who struggled for them. Marshall (1950: 94) comments that the early use of collective bargaining by the trade union movement raised the social and economic status of its members: that is, it established a claim that workers, 'as citizens, were entitled to certain social rights'. Marshall fails to note, however, that significant elements of the trade union movement at the time understood the achievement of social rights in terms of two sets of possibilities, neither of which corresponds with Marshall's usage.

Some participants in the struggle for social rights argued that they could be achieved through high wages and wage-maintenance through full employment; others, who believed that such things were not achievable in capitalism, held that social rights could be attained only through the socialistic overthrow of the market economy (Brown 1983: 42–4; Gallie 1983: 195–205). The view that social rights were realizable through social policy enacted by the existing state was not widely accepted by the British labour movement of seven or eight decades ago. Although by no means universal, the idea that social rights could be achieved only through the socialistic reconstruction of economy and society was much more widespread. Marshall does not consider this aspect of social rights in *Citizenship and Social Class* although he indirectly acknowledges it in later discussion, but without modifying his approach (Marshall 1961: 290; 1961a: 260–6).

As a component of citizenship social rights necessarily entail a direct association with social policy; they 'imply an absolute right to a certain standard of civilization which is *conditional only on the discharge of the general duties of citizenship*' (Marshall 1950: 94; emphasis added). The conditional form of this statement makes it quite clear that struggle against employer and government for entitlements in the labour market must be irrelevant to the attainment of social rights. In this context, then, the struggles of the union movement to achieve improved wages and terms of employment for their members have to be regarded as part of a set of considerations which relate not to 'rights' but to 'conditions'. In addition, it is implicit in Marshall's treatment that the provision of social rights in exchange for the duties of citizenship renders contradictory the idea that social rights can be attained through the struggle for socialism. It remains, then, for the social services of the state to satisfy social rights, which minimally entail the right to a degree of economic welfare and security. It is in this vein that a necessary association of social rights and social policy is implicit.

One view of welfare policy is that it tends to immobilize those who are subject to it. In his discussion in *Society and Democracy in Germany* Ralf Dahrendorf (1969: 70) insists that while social policy has the potential to strengthen the sense of responsibility in citizens and guarantee the status of citizenship, it is also possible that social policy can hold citizens in tutelage. Marshall wrote *Citizenship and Social Class* at least partly in defence of the welfare state that had only a few years earlier been launched by a Labour administration. Perhaps this is why he stresses only the first of these possibilities and uncritically accepts that there can be no contradiction between the attainment of social rights and the practice of the social services. In later discussions, however, Marshall in effect departs from this position when he points to two distinct processes which are mutually reinforcing.

First, in his discussion of 'Value Problems of Welfare-Capitalism', Marshall (1972: 114) acknowledges that 'paternalistic welfare' might undermine a person's sense of independence and initiative, although he seems to doubt that an individual's sense of personal responsibility is necessarily endangered by the state's provision of health-care and education. The significant point here, though, is the recognition that social policy has the capacity to adversely influence the ability of individuals to act on their own behalf and on their own terms. Second, in this textbook, *Social Policy in the Twentieth Century*, Marshall (1975: 206–7) shows that social rights are not necessarily expressed through social policy. According to Marshall's argument here, social *rights* require, among other things, that those who are entitled to benefits or social services know what their rights are and that they are able to lay claim to them.

Marshall elaborates this last point when he goes on to say that '[t]he rights of citizenship are a reality only for those who have belief in their authenticity and the skills needed to exercise them' (Marshall 1975: 207). Thus in a real sense the substance of rights cannot be merely given. If a person simply receives benefits or services as a consequence of a legal status which is not achieved through some exercise of social skill on the recipient's part, it is doubtful that rights are involved. Marshall immediately goes on to add that belief in the authenticity of citizenship rights and the skill required to exercise them 'are developed through experience and socialization in the context of a class society'. One consequence of this is that class inequality constitutes the chief barrier to the fulfilment of the condition that social services express social rights, for any claim to social services, he says, 'can seem to some a mark of status and to others a brand of inferiority'.

Together these points suggest that the relationship between social rights and social policy is problematic. The practice of social policy may undermine the qualities individuals require in order to recognize and exercize rights. This is particularly so in a welfare state where the delivery of social services is dominated by over-worked and under-staffed bureaucracies and professions which, in spite of their best intentions, tend to operate in ways which emphasize the dependent status of their clients. In addition, and more critical for Marshall's general argument, social policies do not necessarily express social rights. In a class society, in which socialization and experience differentially equip persons from different class backgrounds, it is likely that those most in need of social services are least likely to receive them as rights, properly understood. Social rights and social policy are analytically quite distinct, and the empirical relationship between the two is not direct. The idea that there is somehow an inevitable link between social rights and social policy, which is to be found in *Citizenship and Social Class*, cannot be sustained.

When the nexus between social rights and social policy is broken the concept of 'social rights' must play a more limited role in discussion of social policy than Marshall envisages. As social policy does not necessarily express social rights the concept of social rights can no longer be expected to assist a general understanding of the development and function of the social services and educational institutions. At most it can serve as a rod against which particular social policies might be measured. In this context the concept of social rights might be an element in a critique of social policy which asks whether particular policies are in fact expressions of social rights. This is a role rather different from the one implied in social rights as an element of citizenship.

iii

The idea that social rights may form an element of citizenship not only is central to Marshall's account, but has become a part of the common currency of twentieth-century understandings of rights and citizenship. Nevertheless, the proposition that social rights can be rights of citizenship warrants critical examination on at least three grounds. First, citizenship rights are rights of participation in a common national community. Social rights may be required for the practice of citizenship in so far as they enable such participation. But this is precisely to say that as a means of facilitating citizenship they cannot be said to constitute it. Second, citizenship rights are necessarily universal. Social rights, on the other hand, are only meaningful when they are substantive; and substantive rights can never be universal. Finally, social rights are always conditional upon an administrative and professional infrastructure, and ultimately upon a fiscal basis: thus they might be better described not as rights but as conditional opportunities. Each of these issues will be dealt with in turn.

According to Marshall (1950: 92) citizenship requires 'a direct sense of community membership based on loyalty to a civilization which is a common possession'. It would therefore seem to follow that a social component of citizenship can be postulated which includes a range of rights:

> from the right to a modicum of economic welfare and security to the right to share to the full in the social heritage and to live the life of a

civilized being according to the standards prevailing in the society
(1950: 72).

It is for this reason that it is held by Marshall and others that the
full evolutionary development of citizenship is attained through the
realization of its social component. Because citizenship operates as
a principle of equal status, equal participation in social life is at least
a potential aspect of all citizenship. The difficulty with this general
proposition, however, is that it confuses citizenship rights with the
means through which such rights are realized.

Before the historical advent of political rights which extended
political citizenship to the working class, the question of social
rights did not arise. Social rights, in their modern form, were first
advocated by nineteenth-century socialists (Macpherson 1985: 23).
The right to participate in political life, no matter how formal and
limited, will necessarily make less tolerable exclusion from
economic security and well-being. As discussion above indicates,
the generation of policy to secure a modicum of social rights derives
from the dual forces of popular pressures for reform on the one
hand, and of reform to contain popular pressures for change on the
other. Although he fails to fill in the details, Marshall (1950: 74),
after insisting that the different components of citizenship arise
sequentially, goes on to say that political and social rights overlap
significantly in their historical development.

It can be argued, therefore, that social rights appear in order to
redress the tension, between the status of equal participation in
citizenship and the unequal exclusion from economic security,
which is thrown into clear relief by the expansion of political
citizenship. There is no better way of describing the incorporation
of social rights in the status of citizenship than to follow Marshall
(1950: 96) in saying that it creates 'a universal right to real income
that is not proportionate to the market value of the claimant'.

Citizenship rights are rights to equal participation in a national
community, which is an end in itself. The real income achieved
through social rights, on the other hand, cannot be an end but is a
means; in particular, it is a means to share in a 'social heritage'
which includes the exercise of civil and political rights. Income is
sometimes regarded as an 'end' but the real end in this case is the
psychological satisfaction persons derive from their income; which
is to say that in this context as well income has to be regarded as a
means. To say that social right is a right to real income is therefore a
statement of an entirely different order than to say that social right

is a right to participate in a social heritage or common civilization. Ignoring the difficulties of meaningfully specifying what this 'common civilization' might be, if social rights are to be distinguished from the rights associated with the civil and the political components of citizenship, what remains for them can only be rights to the means which will enhance the exercise of civil and political citizenship. Indeed, this is the function or purpose generally ascribed to social rights.

In the absence of the educational and economic resources required to exercise civil or legal and political rights citizenship remains empty for all practical purposes. Social rights, as rights to social services and education, enable citizens to partake in the national community to which their status entitles them. This point is clear in Talcott Parsons' (1965: 260) summary (although some may say reformulation) of Marshall's account of citizenship:

> The social component does not concern the opportunity to express and implement the rights derived from the societal values so much as the resources and capacities necessary for this implementation. In this connection the societal community defines and presents standards for the allocation of resources to the community as a whole and to its various subsectors.

The strong distinction between citizenship rights and rights enabling participation in citizenship, drawn in the preceding discussion and implicit in the quotation above, would have limited significance if it were not for the fact that from the perspective of citizenship rights the social component is defective on other grounds as well.

In his general discussion of them Marshall describes social rights as universal, as indeed he must if they are to be regarded as citizenship rights. But when he comes to treat them in detail Marshall (1950: 97–106) shows that the difference between individual needs is such that access to particular social services is far from universal. Marshall does not see this as necessarily contradictory, for there can be a general commitment on the part of the state to reduce risk and insecurity in the community as a whole. In this sense the *right* to social services can be described as universal. Marshall goes so far as to suggest that it is possible to say that, subject to considerations of cost, the provision of certain services can in practice be universal. Yet the requirement that those who wish to exercise their rights to social services will have to meet particular qualifying criteria casts doubt on whether universal rights can actually be said to operate. The tension between the obligation of the state towards society as a whole and the individual claims for social services is treated by Marshall (1950: 104–5; 1953: 237; 1975: 206) as a consequence of the finite nature of stocks of resources. This is a problem, certainly. It will be examined below. But this is not the only aspect of the issue.

The state may be committed to providing social services as a right to all citizens. But social services, unlike equality before the law, for instance, and political participation, are only meaningful in terms of the particular services themselves. The full implication of this is that it becomes difficult if not impossible to treat social rights as having any universality. In another context Roberto Unger (1976: 198) argues that '[n]o matter how substantive justice is defined it can be achieved only by treating different situations differently'. It must follow, then, that in order to be meaningful universal social rights are required to satisfy individually different needs. Of course this conclusion is contradictory: universal rights do not require but countermand individual preferences. More to the point for our present purposes, social services have to be particular because social and economic disabilities are by their nature particular.

Civil rights, on the other hand, can readily be universal citizenship rights because formal equality before the law can meaningfully be achieved for all through the establishment of legal institutions, irrespective of the individual condition. Political rights can also be universal rights of citizenship because formal access to political participation can be provided by simply instituting popular suffrage, for instance, without regard to individual conditions. But social rights cannot provide economic security on a universal basis because economic security is not amenable to formal expression in the way that equality before the law and political participation are. The idea of universal social rights must remain amorphous precisely because social services have to be tailored to particular needs (Weber 1921: 886). For this reason some regulation concerning the conditions of access is required of social services. Without it the benefits and services would be inefficient and ineffectual in their operation. But with it the equality of status required of citizenship rights is negated.

The third difficulty with social rights as citizenship rights is that they are fiscally conditional. Marshall (1969: 141) says that social rights refer to individuals not as actors but as consumers. He could have added that the consumption implicit in social rights does not eliminate the concept of actor and in fact requires it, but in the form of the state rather than of the human subject. This is because the goods and services consumed through the operation of social rights are provided and guaranteed by the state. Unlike civil and political rights social rights in citizenship require certain distributional activities of the state. The provision of social services and transfer payments involve the state in an expenditure which is not required in the provision of the other rights constituting modern citizenship. And they require an administrative structure for the delivery of social services which itself adds to the financial costs of social rights.

It is true that civil and political rights also require state institutions and activity for their realization. Legal and representative arrangements, institutions and processes are constructed by the state and become aspects of it. Such institutions both provide the basis of civil and political rights, and set limitations on them. But once in place these institutions themselves more or less constitute the material bases of the rights with which they are associated, and while they are not financially cost-free, their fiscal basis has never featured in any calculation of their feasibility. This is not the case with social rights, however.

The provision of social services as a right is necessarily conditional on the capacity of the fiscal basis of the state to pay for such services. In the early history of social services, during the first three decades of this century, the under-developed means of procuring revenue enforced a modesty on state expenditure and therefore on the services the state could provide to its citizens. The changes in economic policy, which are associated with the Keynesian 'revolution', permitted an increase in the amount of revenue available to the state and assured the growth of the social services as well as enhancing the arguments that their scope be extended. It follows that the institutions associated with social rights are not only the social services but also the fiscal arrangements which sustain them. Marshall (1950: 104) acknowledges that the rate of progress in the provision of social rights 'depends on the magnitude of the national resources and their distribution between competing claims'. The significance of this qualification is that the relationship between the institutional basis of social rights and the rights themselves is necessarily unstable.

Once representative institutions are in place formal political rights are more or less secure, other things being equal. An analogous situation does not hold for the relationship between the fiscal basis of social security and social rights. There are two elements in this argument. First, the demand for social rights is a demand for services and benefits which will always be ahead of their supply. This is a factor Marshall (1950: 104) recognizes when he says that:

> the State [cannot] easily foresee what it will cost to fulfil its obligations, for, as the standard expected of the services rises – as it inevitably must in a progressive society – the obligations automatically get heavier. The target is perpetually moving forward, and the state may never be able to get within range of it.

While Marshall is aware of this first point he seems to be unaware of a second, namely, that the fiscal basis on which social security rests is itself dependent on an economic environment which is constantly subject not only to change but to forces in the international economy which the nation-state can never control. In both these respects the bases of social rights are wholly unlike those of the legal and political components of citizenship. For these and other reasons given above, social rights can never be more than secondary rights of citizenship, as Marshall understands the term.

iv

The idea that there is a basic conflict between the principle of social rights and the principle of the market is central to Marshall's treatment of changes in capitalist society resulting from the historic enlargement of citizenship through the advent of the welfare state. A radical reading of this proposition, holding that social rights undermine the market and market relations, is supported by some of Marshall's formulations, as we have seen a number of times in earlier chapters. This perspective resonates with a view, widely expressed today, that the market economy is threatened by government expenditure on social services and education. We shall return to this matter below. For the present it is necessary to clarify the idea in Marshall's thought that there is some form of opposition between the principles of social right and market.

As we have already seen, Marshall defines social rights in opposition to market relations. But there are at least two qualifications in Marshall's discussion in *Citizenship and Social Class* which should lead to a more cautious interpretation of his general claim than is frequently encountered in the literature. Marshall

(1950: 71) does insist that the basic equality of modern citizenship cannot be 'created and preserved without invading the freedom of the competitive market'. He goes on to say, though, 'that it is equally obvious that the market still functions – within limits'. The qualification is gratuitous as all markets necessarily function within limits. Markets themselves never determine what type of resource is to be subject to market forces or available outside market exchanges, and markets themselves can never provide the institutional infrastructure required for their functioning. These and other pre-conditions of markets and market activity, which are therefore limits on the scope and operation of markets, are provided by non-market power relations and especially by legislation and state activity. Marshall seems not unaware of this point for he goes on to suggest that it is always necessary to specify the special limitations imposed on markets by social rights. Thus when Marshall immediately adds that here there is only a '*possible* conflict of principles which demands examination' (emphasis added) he implicitly acknowledges that the conflict between social rights and markets is not even certain.

The idea that there is a fundamental contradiction between social rights and market exchanges is further qualified in a way which even more clearly weakens the radical interpretation of their relation. Marshall (1950: 111) says that:

> Social rights in their modern form imply an invasion of contract by status, the subordination of market price to social justice, the replacement of the free bargain by the declaration of rights.

Here rights and market are opposites. But he immediately goes on to say that they are at the same time continuous:

> But are these principles quite foreign to the practice of the market today, or are they there already, entrenched within the contract system itself? I think that it is clear that they are.

Marshall demonstrates this notion in a treatment of the growth of trade unionism and its consequences on the development of citizenship. The implication here is that the growth of citizenship in a market society is endogenous. These matters have been treated in various places above and there is no need to deal with them again here. Marshall (1950: 113) moves on to a discussion of the wage structure in labour markets and considers the prevailing conception of what constitutes a fair wage in order to demonstrate his general point further. He concludes that a fair wage contains not only an understanding of market value but also 'a notion of status'. In particular, the claims to status in wage determination are to a 'hierarchical wage structure, each level of which represents a social right and not merely a market value'. In this discussion social right can be found more or less harmoniously within the market. The rights Marshall is discussing here are not citizenship rights, certainly. But they are normative principles of distribution, which function with market principles in setting wage rates.

The influence of social as opposed to economic factors in the determination of wage rates has been noticed by other writers. Jan Pen (1974: 100), for instance, proposes that:

> The wage structure is the result of a network of two groups of forces which is not easy to disentangle. It is not even easy to establish whether the income of one given income recipient . . . is determined by 'economic' forces or by the system of social values.

Pen (1974: 99) does say, though, that 'as a rule the status value prevails as one rises in the wage structure.' The view that wage rates can be explained by status rather than merely market forces has been strenuously advocated by Barbara Wootton, *The Social Foundations of Wages Policy* (1955). Wootton (1955: 64) observes that a most consistent feature of the British wage structure is that 'those who give orders should normally be better paid than those to whom such orders are given'. This observation is relevant to an understanding of Pen's formulation above, for it suggests that whether a status claim is efficacious in determining wages depends on whether it corresponds to the degree of authority or power associated with the job to which the earnings are attached. It could be argued, therefore, that occupational status, or rights, emerges from a distribution of power, and that labour market power can become legitimated as a status right. Such a situation is an instance of a more general tendency (Weber 1921: 213). It emerges from this discussion that if the competitive preservation of privilege is normal in market exchanges, then it is likely that status rights will work with market principles in determining the structure of pay.

The conclusions to be drawn from this are that while social rights and market value are in many ways opposed to each other, the opposition between them is not necessarily fundamental and that in fact they may work together in contributing to a single outcome. Such a situation would ordinarily be described as a division of labour, and this is a possible characterization of the relationship between social rights and the market economy. This is arguably the way in which Marshall perceives the relationship between them, even though he never expresses it directly in these terms.

A division of labour is essentially a situation of cooperation between two or more factors which are able to effect a single outcome by virtue of the different contributions each can make. This notion preserves the idea that social rights on the one hand and the market on the other can be defined as opposites, while at the same time it underscores the continuation of market relations after the advent of social rights in citizenship, and also the contribution of both rights and market value in the structure of earnings, for example. According to this understanding of the relationship between social rights and the market the rise of the welfare state implies not the collapse of the market economy but its modification or complementation, such that the satisfaction of needs is met from more then one source. This is a quite different appreciation of the significance of social citizenship for market relations than the view that they are fundamentally opposed and 'at war' with each other.

The overall impression created by Marshall in *Citizenship and Social Class* is that the rise of social rights spells the decline or at least the shrinking of the market and market relations. But there are other statements which lead to the qualification of such an impression, as indicated above. In later works the suggestion that there is a division of labour between social citizenship and market relations is much more clearly implied. It is strongest in Marshall's idea of a 'hyphenated society', spelled out in 'Value Problems of Welfare-Capitalism' and its 'Afterthought'. In the latter Marshall (1981a: 133) says that:

> It is legitimate, and also profitable, to regard welfare and the market as embodying two different ways of performing the same task, that of satisfying the needs and wants of the population. That being so, it is obviously important to decide how this complex task should be shared between them.

That social rights and market values can together contribute to the satisfaction of needs and wants may not be difficult to accept although it should not be taken for granted. An issue for an understanding of the welfare state, and Marshall's treatment of it, therefore, is whether and how the provision of resources from one source in fact affects the operation of the other source.

One aspect of the relationship between state provision and

the market economy which Marshall wholly ignores is the way in which the market provision of social insurance can seriously undermine the effectiveness of social security as a social right (Titmuss 1958; Sinfield 1978). This blind spot is the obverse of Marshall's insistence that the line of vulnerability is in the other direction, that citizenship rights encroach on market practices. On this ground Marshall's hyphenated-society model does not much improve the one developed in *Citizenship and Social Class*; private or market insurance and social insurance do not simply divide the labour of providing social security but in fact are in competition to do so. This type of situation may not have arisen for Marshall's exemplar of non-market provision through social right, the British National Health Service, at the time of his writing *Citizenship and Social Class*. But consideration of this case raises another problem.

When the Labour Government established the National Health Service in 1946 with legislation to take effect from 1948 two serious problems faced British health care: the voluntary hospital sector was effectively bankrupt (Klein 1983: 4) and scientific medicine was in a phase of technical change which brought in new equipment and treatments (Klein 1983: 14). The combination of these factors meant that health costs were high and inflationary. With the socialization of medicine through the NHS the budgetary units expanded overnight and investment in plant and equipment could be more readily achieved. In other words, by removing the consumption of medical services from the market place, the market in medical capital equipment was secured and could expand. Here, then, the non-market provision of medical services is significantly driven by the expansion of costs in the market of medical capital goods. It should be added that while the socialization of medicine reduced the market in medical services it could not remove it. To the degree that private medicine was available to the economically privileged the universality of medical care as a citizenship right was diminished.

A prevalent view today is that for the market economy to function at all effectively the welfare state has to be cut back. The underlying assumption of this position is in effect accepted by the radical interpretation of Marshall's claim that the principles of social citizenship and the market are opposed. The history of the post-war welfare state can be characterized in terms of its evolving contradiction with the market economy. During the 1950s and 1960s the general consensus was that the welfare state enhanced the operation of the market economy by both stabilizing it and raising its productiveness. From the 1970s, however, the welfare state and the market economy have increasingly been on a collision course. Unlike most progressive liberal and social-democratic advocates of the welfare state Marshall was always aware of an underlying tension between state provision and the market. It is possible, therefore, that in this regard at least Marshall has contributed to our general understanding of the welfare state.

In the closing sentences of *Citizenship and Social Class* Marshall (1950: 122) draws attention to the potential, indeed impending unstable relationship between what he here describes as the *principle* of citizenship and the *principle* of the market. More recently Marshall (1972), referring not to principles but to *values*, returned to this theme of the potential contradiction between welfare and the market. The earlier work is marked by a certain vagueness about how the tension between welfare and market is checked, except in so far as Marshall (1950: 122) says that stability is 'achieved through a compromise which is not dictated by logic.' Perhaps it is because of such formulations that commentators have turned instead to the discussion in 'Value Problems of Welfare-Capitalism' in order to follow Marshall's reasoning on the tension between welfare provision and market exchange, where the matter is treated in more detail. The difficulty, however, is that while most commentators have assumed that Marshall's arguments in the two works are more or less continuous, the institutional focus of *Citizenship and Social Class* is in a significant sense lost in 'Value Problems of Welfare-Capitalism'.

According to his discussion in the later work Marshall (1972: 119) sees the tension between the welfare sector and the market economy as inevitable precisely because he believes that each must be defined in value terms and that different values are necessarily non-commensurable. But Marshall is confident that the resulting tension is not necessarily destructive of the balance between the different components of the mixed economy, or, as he prefers, the hyphenated society. In his 'Afterthought' on this discussion Marshall (1981a: 129) comments that 'it would be absurd to assume that the coexistence of different value systems in different contexts must necessarily be on balance "dysfunctional", since this kind of ethical relativity has been a feature of very nearly every society since civilization began'. He goes on to indicate that the difference between the welfare sector and the market economy should therefore be seen as analogous to the differences between the family and the community, for instance, or between the military and the civilian; each is founded on different values but as complementary parts of a whole. This leads Marshall (1972: 120) to argue that the current endeavours of Western governments to economize on welfare is simply an aspect of transient 'capitalist alarmism' which is 'unlikely to be built into the system'. His solution to the tension of value differences is in terms of 'better two-way communications' so that the different role of each sector can be better understood and the clear division of labour between them maintained.

Any analysis of the welfare state based on an assumption that institutions can be summarized in terms of the values they are supposed to exemplify is bound to be sociologically limited in the extreme. Marshall's (1972: 109) claim that welfare decisions 'must draw on standards of value embodied in an autonomous ethical system' not only moves away from the more concrete analysis of *Citizenship and Social Class*, which focuses instead on practices and institutions as material realities, but fails to appreciate that values *are* trans-institutional. It is precisely as a projection of political and economic values that Bismarckian, Lloyd Georgian and Beveridgian welfare institutions came into being.

These limitations of Marshall's approach should not lead us to accept the argument of those who criticize him for paying insufficient attention to the relationship between the welfare sector on the one hand and capital accumulation, international economic competition and similar matters on the other. While any treatment of the welfare state would benefit enormously by taking such things into consideration, it must be said that in showing the limitations of Marshall's analysis in this regard his critics (Hindess 1987: 35; Macpherson 1985: 26; Turner 1986: 48–9) have been too ready to accept that the state provision of welfare does in fact inhibit the development of the capitalist market.

There are types and levels of welfare provision that are widely accepted as 'functional' for capitalist economies. What types and what levels will vary with different sorts of economy and with different phases of their development. For instance, one function of state welfare through which operation of the market economy is enhanced is in the maintenance of a level of consumption which will tend to flatten out the boom-slump cycle in the economy. It has been suggested in a different context that if the spending capacity of the American work-force during the 1930s had been greater the Depression would have been less profound and shorter. This type of argument may have less relevance for export-oriented economies than it does for those in which the domestic market has an important bearing on economic activity. However none of this indicates that a state's welfare spending would be a 'burden' in one context where it would not be in another. It simply indicates that a function which may be significant in one context may be redundant in another.

The distinction between the political intentions of capitalists on the one hand and the technical requirements of the capitalist economy on the other is difficult to maintain in practical terms. But analytically it is crucial for showing that any suggestion that welfare spending inhibits the development and operation of the capitalist market economy has no necessary basis and is likely to be a short-term political demand rather than a technical economic imperative. In his discusson of what in effect is the sociology of business confidence Michael Kalecki (1943) has shown that the business community is able to exercise political leverage over economic decision-making, and indirectly over the government, if the level of employment in an economy is predominantly a consequence of private investment. For this reason business is opposed to government expenditure, including that which subsidizes consumption, which is the economic function of social security.

As it is stated here Kalecki's generalization is possibly too bold, for there are circumstances under which employers as a class are prepared not to campaign against social security and welfare measures. But when they feel it is in their interests to do so, campaigns against government expenditure on welfare and education will be mounted for what are essentially short-term purposes without proper reference to the middle or long-term consequences for the economy as a whole. It is more probably this type of situation which faces the Western welfare states today than an inevitable technically based contradiction between state expenditure and capital accumulation.

Neither Marshall nor his critics have much to offer for an analysis of the welfare state whose present problems and course of development are not readily mastered either by the assumption that social services and the market are necessarily opposed or by the assumption that they are involved in a harmonious division of labour for the satisfaction of social needs.

6

Citizenship in Political and Social Integration

The degree to which political and social actions conform with established practices and are consistent with the actions of others (rather than in conflict with them) is the extent to which it can be said that there is political and social integration. The individuals and groups implicated in such processes are thereby 'incorporated' or 'integrated' into a unified social system. This terminology may be contentious, either because it is thought to assume functionally inter-related parts and therefore a 'system' in a reified sense, or else a manipulative dominant class, stratum or group able to achieve the compliance of those socially and politically subordinate to it. There are elements of these factors in different accounts of social integration, certainly. But there is no need for these considerations to prejudice our use of the notion. Integration can simply be understood as a term which refers to a situation in which inter-actions are not disruptive of a set of more or less stable and enduring relationships in which individuals and groups are involved.

One approach holds that integration is achieved when action is guided by a common set of norms and values. This position, generally associated with the work of Talcott Parsons, emphasizes the systemic and functional nature of fundamental values. While it is feasible that the achievement of integration may tend to promote a general adherence to a more or less common set of norms or values it cannot be accepted that social integration is attained through the operation of a common value system. When social conditions and opportunities are unequally distributed correspond-ing different sets of values and expectations tend to arise. These cannot be part of a unified system, for what is valued as advantage for some will be seen as disadvantage for others.

A second possibility focuses not on values but on material

benefits. When interest groups or their representatives are able to bargain and negotiate with each other and reach agreement on distributional exchanges, for instances, some form of pragmatic equilibrium may be achieved which, though limited and temporary, will be regarded by those participating in it as part of a framework through which at least some advantages will accrue to each of them. Such social exchanges in which more or less all social interests are involved will tend to lead to a general satisfaction with existing arrangements. Under these conditions goals which may be disruptive of existing arrangements are less likely to be pursued and more likely to be displaced, if other interests are satisfied.

A third possibility is that persons and groups come to accept a given situation and therefore come to be socially integrated if they lack the means to alter or change it. Emile Durkheim (1893: 356) expresses this view when he says that 'the working classes are not really satisfied with the conditions under which they live, but very often accept them only as constrained and forced, since they have not the means to change them'.

Citizenship, as equal participation in a national community, is one means of achieving social and political integration, either through the general acceptance of common values or through the negation of divisive inequalities. Whilst it is difficult to avoid a role for citizenship in an account of social and political integration, it is necessary to add that citizenship rights cannot be regarded only as an integrative force. There are a number of reasons for avoiding an identity of citizenship with social integration. First, citizenship rights have been the focus of social conflict and not just the basis of social harmony. Second, it would be difficult to maintain that those governments which diminish the scope of citizenship – by dismantling the welfare apparatus of the state, for example – are thereby undermining social integration. This raises a more general caution. To say that integrative processes are operating is not to say that contradictory processes have no reality, that society is a coherent whole, stable and unchanging.

i

Marshall's account of citizenship has come to be regarded as crucially important for its contribution to our understanding of social integration (Lockwood 1974: 365–6; Halsey 1984: 13). It is Marshall's emphasis on the principle of equality in citizenship rights which, according to these accounts, provides an explanation of the institutional basis for social cohesion and solidarity. Indeed, Lockwood and Halsey go so far as to say that Marshall's treatment of integration is more complete and satisfactory than that found in the classical sociology of Emile Durkheim and Max Weber. Not only is this aspect of Marshall's treatment of citizenship less developed and coherent than Lockwood's and Halsey's assessments suggest, it is not the only basis of social integration in Marshall's account of citizenship.

Most commentators have failed to notice the importance Marshall gives to the duties or obligations of citizenship, and their role in the maintenance of social order and integration, although Morris Janowitz (1980) is an exception here. Indeed, in *Citizenship and Social Class* Marshall (1950: 112) declares that '[i]f citizenship is invoked in the defence of rights, the corresponding duties of citizenship cannot be ignored'. This has particular relevance in the area of industrial citizenship, according to Marshall, in which he holds that rights have to be subordinate to duties, as we saw in Chapter 2. This aspect of citizenship, and especially its general role in the integration of society, is rather more dominant and much more forcefully expressed in Marshall's earlier paper, 'Work and Wealth', which rehearses some of the arguments more fully expressed in *Citizenship and Social Class*, but to which Janowitz does not refer. In 'Work and Wealth' Marshall (1945: 218–9) insists on the importance of loyalty to the state and goes so far as to suggest that the role of propaganda in achieving it should not be ignored.

Yet Janowitz does overstate the importance of duties in Marshall's argument. While Marshall regards duty as critical in the operation of particular elements of citizenship, as we have just indicated, its role in the practice of citizenship in general is limited by the fact that 'the national community is too large and remote to command this kind of loyalty and to make it a continual driving force' (Marshall 1950: 119). Marshall's account of the duties of citizenship cannot be ignored when his contribution to the theory of integration is raised. But it is entirely secondary to his treatment of citizenship rights. Indeed, this is the more interesting aspect of the treatment of integration precisely because it transcends the conventional basis of social cohesion, solidarity and integration in terms of the obligatory aspects of social institutions.

ii

The importance of the political rights of citizenship and especially the suffrage are almost universally regarded as central to the integrative process, although it is interesting to note that they are given a relatively low priority by Marshall in this regard. The more appropriate reference here is Reinhard Bendix's interpretation and development of Marshall's treatment of citizenship. Bendix (1964: 73) argues that in attempting to overcome its economic and political subordination in early modern European society, the rising working class was not led to overthrow the old and seek a new social order, but instead demanded entry to the political community of the nation state, and the right of equal participation in it. It is the success of these endeavours, Bendix says, which explains both the decline of socialism as a political force in the Western working-class movements and the integration of the lower classes in Western societies.

The basic assumptions of this argument are that the intention of directed popular agitation was the expansion of the franchise and political citizenship, and that this is central to the integrative process. These points are so widely held they can be regarded as axioms of political sociology. So basic are these propositions that the failure of Marxists to accept them has been taken to indicate the limitations of their approach (Turner 1986). In fact this test is confounded in a way which more surely demonstrates the certainty of the premises it defends: these points are expounded by Marxists themselves. Ellen Wood (1986: 148–50), for instance, argues that political democracy or citizenship is 'the legacy of historic struggles by subordinate classes', that its achievements in 'civilizing capitalist exploitation' and providing 'new possibilities of organization and resistance' for subordinate classes are real, and therefore that the acceptance of liberal-democratic political forms 'cannot be lightly dismissed as a failure of class-consciousness or a betrayal of the revolution', and that in those countries in which the traditions of parliamentary democracy have been strongest the struggle for socialist revolution 'means putting at risk hard-won gains for the sake of uncertain benefits'.

A recognition that universal suffrage and representative institutions can enhance the opportunities and conditions of the working class need not deny that these same institutions can stabilize the existing social order and serve its dominant class by helping to channel and reduce popular pressure and conflict. It will be shown in this section and the next, however, that there is a tendency in such arguments to over-emphasize the extent and significance of working-class agitation in the expansion of the suffrage, and to do so at the cost of ignoring anti-parliamentarist tendencies within the working-class movement (Young 1967). In addition, such arguments exaggerate the degree to which political integration was achieved historically through suffrage, and also misleadingly insist that political reform was won by the subordinate classes at the expense of the dominant or ruling class.

The Second Reform Bill of 1867 is of signal importance to arguments concerning the role of the suffrage in the integrative process because it is generally held that the political incorporation of the English working class was more or less achieved through its enactment. The First Reform Bill of 1832 left five out of six adult males without the vote. This situation was significantly altered by the reforms of 1867. The immediate effect of the 1867 Bill was to increase the electorate from one to two and a half million voters and, because it gave the franchise to all householders in Parliamentary Boroughs, to include urban working-class men in the suffrage. But the picture created by these facts requires qualifications which are too seldom given to it. First, while the 1867 Bill changed the situation of those who lived in the mainly urban boroughs, it left unaffected those who lived in the mainly rural counties. Thus agricultural workers and certain categories of industrial workers, including a large proportion of miners, were left voteless. Second, as H. F. Moorhouse has shown, the enfranchisement of the working class in 1867 has been greatly exaggerated. Moorhouse (1973: 345) presents figures which show that 'after the acts of 1867–8 at best *only* 30% of the male, adult, urban working class were enfranchised'.

The Reform Acts of 1884–5 made the county franchise the same as that of the towns, thus giving the vote to farm labourers and previously excluded miners, and redistributed parliamentary seats. The electorate was increased through these Acts from approximately three to five million; but the population of Britain at the time was 31.4 million. It is only with the Representation of the People Act of 1918 that the adult population (with the exception of women under thirty) was given the vote. Moorhouse (1973: 346) estimates that prior to the 1918 Act only half of the male urban working class was included in the franchise.

It is very difficult to see how the suffrage could effectively function in the political integration of the working class prior to 1918. The fractional admission from 1867 of sections of the male working class had an integrative intention, certainly. But it proceeded precisely by denying suffrage to the working class as a whole and especially to those sections of it which it was feared would have a disruptive influence on the political system if they were included in it. To say this does not deny that political rights were extended during the nineteenth century in Britain. Yet even though the 1918 Act attached political rights to citizenship rather than to property, it should not be forgotten that this transition was by no means complete at the time as the different status of men and women under thirty and plural voting remained to be eliminated until universal franchise was instituted in 1928 and equal franchise in 1948.

Marshall (1950: 93) accepts the conventional exaggeration of the extent of the nineteenth-century franchise, but at the same time is clearly aware of the limitations of nineteenth-century electoral reform from the perspective of citizenship rights (1950: 78). He implicitly disagrees that the extension of the franchise from the time of the 1867 Bill exercised an integrative influence over the working class by failing to discuss it at all in that context, and in this regard is quite unlike Bendix, and many others. Nevertheless, Marshall (1950: 93) does distort the situation somewhat when he says that the 'political rights of citizenship . . . were full of potential danger to the capitalist system, although those who were cautiously extending them down the social scale probably did not realize quite how great the danger was'.

In fact electoral and political reform was conducted by the British Establishment with full anticipation of its likely outcome. Extension of the suffrage was sponsored by political parties in government and carefully consolidated as it proceeded so that the sections of the population newly integrated with each new legislative development did not threaten the political system they had been allowed to enter. In the years immediately following the Second Reform Bill, for instance, a system of public elementary education was established, the Civil Service and the army were reorganized and the law was overhauled so that many of its Dickensian elements were removed (Cole and Postgate 1946: 365–6). The argument here does not deny the reality of the struggle for the vote and the fight for political rights by the Chartists and the labour movement in general. What has to be kept in focus, though, is that the initiative for reform was with the ruling class, which acted out of self-interest, and which instituted only those changes which preserved its position of privilege. Raph Miliband (1984: 25) aptly summarizes the situation when he says that in 'the context of a solid parliamentary and political system decisively shaped by the forces of property, the extension of the suffrage was more an act of containment than of emancipation.'

Moorhouse (1973: 345) shows that the debates preceding the 1867 reforms were based on detailed statistical and political appraisals of the effects of various legislative proposals. He goes on to show that these and other nineteenth-century reforms had the purpose of serving the interests and electoral chances of established political parties and not primarily of extending the rights of citizens. The new urban proletariat was regarded as a threat by the ruling class and it was thought that its piecemeal and selective political incorporation would reduce the possibility of violent revolution. The means and manner through which this was accomplished changed institutional forms but not the differential distribution of power in society. Bendix (1964: 100) shows how the secret ballot, for instance, introduced in England in 1872, neutralized the threat of emergent working-class organizations by isolating the individual working-class voter not simply from his superiors but more importantly from his peers.

To the extent that political integration was achieved through the expansion of the franchise during the nineteenth century it succeeded by structurally limiting the options of the new voters. Those who controlled the sources of economic and political power determined the nature of the franchise and the alternatives available through it (Moorhouse 1973: 353). It will be clear from this why Simon Clarke (1982: 133) argues that:

> The extension of the franchise was not intended to admit the working class to the constitution, but to bring into the electoral game those who exhibited moral reliability and political responsibility, qualities measured by respect for property and the constitution and found among the more affluent, and correspondingly improved, sections of the working class, but which were defined in moral and not in economic terms. Citizenship and not property was to become the basis of political representation. The extension of the franchise was seen as the necessary framework for political alliances that would transcend class, and so as the only viable alternative to class struggle.

The political incorporation of the British working class, and therefore the integration of British society, was not achieved through the slow and controlled extension of the franchise. Rather, this provided only the necessary background to the historically subsequent routinization of industrial conflict and to the Labour Party's full membership of the parliamentary party system: these are firmer bases of working-class integration. Neither were possible in Britain until after 1918. In order to consolidate the stable institutionalization of industrial relations there had to be a clear and public understanding of the difference between 'good' and 'bad' or acceptable and unacceptable union behaviour, and supporters of the latter had to be isolated from the union movement as a whole. This process was partly achieved in the crucial post-World War I period, as Keith Middlemas (1979: 131–2) shows, through the use and manipulation of the press, by secret government organizations, and by the use of force against unions. Middlemas (1979: 168) goes on to show that as soon as the Labour Party chose its future as an organization for the capture of political power, as it did from the 1920s, it 'claimed, as much as employers or Conservative Party, a vested interest in preserving and enhancing the country's governing institutions'. It is here rather than in the right to vote that political integration is on a sure footing.

iii

To the degree that there is an integrative function in citizenship rights it principally derives from the equality of status which inheres in them. The potentially divisive and socially disruptive inequalities of material condition lose their significance in consequence of the equal participation in the community of citizenship. Marshall (1950: 70) says that 'the inequality of the social class system may be accepted provided the equality of citizenship is recognized'. The capacity of the citizenship status to diminish the significance of potentially disruptive social inequality derives from the real effect of citizenship on inequality itself, according to Marshall. This interaction between citizenship and class is never final; inequality cannot be wholly overcome by citizenship, and to that extent integration can never be complete or finished. This last point will be taken up in the following section.

Citizenship has a role in the integration of society because it has a special significance for participation in social life. For Marshall citizenship is not merely an equalization of rights in a formal sense but involves something much more substantial; it is real member-ship of a real community. For Marshall (1950: 93) citizenship requires 'a direct sense of community membership based on loyalty to a civilization which is a common possession'. A ready interpretation of this statement emphasizes the normative component of citizenship in which individuals as citizens are linked through their acceptance of national and societal values. It will be seen that this is an inadequate summary of Marshall's position, and therefore an inadequate ground on which to reject Marshall's account. Nevertheless, it must be added that Marshall (1972: 109) at times encourages such a reading when, in 'Value Problems of Welfare-Capitalism' for instance, he postulates an 'autonomous ethical system' in the social structure from which welfare decisions are drawn.

The notion of 'civilization' in particular in Marshall's treatment of citizenship requires close examination. Barry Hindess (1987: 39) finds little merit in Marshall's use of the concept of citizenship because, among other things, it is difficult to identify a 'civilization' which is a common possession. Certainly Marshall is quite vague about what comprises the common civilization shared by citizens, although, as we shall see, not quite so vague as sometimes suggested. And yet in this instance vagueness is not necessarily a fault. Although Marshall does not make the point himself it could be argued that the looser the notion of the common civilization shared by citizens the more likely it is that citizenship will be a successful source or support of social integration; the vaguer the idea of a common civilization the greater the range and diversity of interests and values to be accommodated by it. This supposition is particularly interesting in the present context because it requires the opposite of the conventional idea about the nature of values and norms in the integrative process. If values are to integrate social systems, social agents have to 'internalize ' them, and for this to be possible they have to be less than vague. But the 'civilization' Marshall refers to is not of values or norms at all.

The civilization to which Marshall refers is a material civilization which has cultural and social consequences. In the modern class system, which Marshall says emerges out of the declining feudal classes largely through the development of a citizenship based on civil rights, the difference between class cultures practically disappears. This means that the working classes, according to Marshall (1950: 85), 'are provided with a cheap and shoddy imitation of a *civilization that has become national*' [emphasis added]. Coterminous with the birth of civil rights in the eighteenth century and the development of national institutions is a modern national consciousness, the 'first stirrings of a sense of community membership and common heritage' (Marshall 1950: 93). Although Marshall does not spell this out clearly, these two processes are mutually reinforcing and both have clear integrative implications. The issue of a common material civilization will be taken up shortly.

Historiography since Marshall (in particular the work of Asa Briggs, Royden Harrison, Christopher Hill, R. Hilton, E. J. Hobsbawm, John Saville, and E. P. Thompson) suggests that his account of the development of the English – let alone British – national community is misleading. Nigel Young (1967), in summarizing this more recent research, shows, among other things, that the working class has not been integrated into a national culture, and that during the period Marshall refers to the English 'people' were not welded into a national civic unity sharing a common identity or consciousness. The basis of the 'sense of community' Marshall (1950: 92) refers to in particular is eighteenth-century 'patriotic nationalism' and 'jingo patriotism'. In fairness to Marshall's account, it should be mentioned that he does acknowledge that it is difficult to tell how deep or widespread these sentiments were.

It is not necessary to make too strong a case in the other direction in order to clarify the historical situation and correct the impression created by Marshall's brief comments on the acceptance of a common social heritage. An English national identity or consciousness can be traced to the development of a national language in the fourteenth century; and national political institutions were in place, encouraged by foreign war against the French and Dutch, and foreign invasion by the Spanish, by the sixteenth century. But other forces were also at work. With the rise of both capitalist production and the ideology of political economy the customary and traditional supports of life and labour were being pulled down. The 'master's' responsibility to his 'servant' was anathema to the emerging economy, and legislation during the sixteenth and seventeenth centuries cut the common people adrift from the surety to which they had been entitled up until that time. The breakdown and destruction of traditional ties and supports led not only to the alienation of the common people from landlord and manufacturer and to a polarization between the classes, but also to serious and widespread civic dissaffection which was the antithesis of social integration (see Bendix 1974: 34–99).

The increasing awareness of national institutions by the common people during the eighteenth and first half of the nineteenth centuries contained a significant element of resistance to the agencies of central authority which were growing during this period. Young (1967: 10–11) says that:

> It was not merely the direct agencies of social control, troops and police that met opposition, but also officials such as the poor law commissioners provoked deep antagonisms. This period is remarkable for its combination of both a strengthened central authority, and intense social antagonisms with exceptional local volatility. But it was not until the 1840s with new forms of social control (the police, artillery) and rapid transportation (the railways) that this volatility was firmly contained. Until then the dominant sense was one of the fragility of social coordination.

Thus the dominant civic experience and politicization during this period did not lead to civic integration but to its opposite. It is likely that a widespread and integrative nationalism did not emerge in Britain until the period just prior to and during the First World War, and it was at the beginning of the twentieth century that an integrative civic culture emerged, partly sponsored by the parliamentary incorporation of the labour movement. Even today in Britain, with clear class differences in language, diet, manners and customs, and education, it is difficult to say that cultural integration has yet been consolidated (Young 1967: 14–8).

In fact Marshall does not expect too much of the civic and national integration he mistakenly assumed had developed from the eighteenth century because it 'did not have any material effect on class structure and social inequality' (Marshall 1950: 93). The significance of this remark is that it indicates that he believes that the 'common civilization' on which integrative citizenship is based is a material one. Marshall (1950: 96) is quite clear that, among other things:

> mass production for the home market and a growing interest on the part of industry in the needs and tastes of the common people enabled the less well-to-do to enjoy a material civilization which differed less markedly in quality from that of the rich than it had ever done before. All this profoundly altered the setting in which the progress of citizenship took place. Social integration spread from the sphere of sentiment and patriotism into that of material enjoyment. The components of a civilized and cultured life, formerly the monopoly of the few, were brought progressively within reach of the many . . .

It is quite clear from this that for Marshall the notion of a civilized life or a common civilization is the common material culture promoted by mass production. In fact Marshall (1950: 102) refers to 'a general enrichment of the concrete substance of civilized life' in terms of 'a general reduction of risk and insecurity, and equalization between the more and the less fortunate at all levels'. In addition, Marshall (1950: 119) says that the 'unified civilization which makes social inequalities acceptable, and threatens to make them economically functionless, is achieved by a progressive divorce between real and money incomes'. But the advent of mass production in the economy has a context in the class nature of modern society. This is a contributing factor to the integrative role of modern citizenship.

Marshall's point is that while citizenship in general tends to promote a common trans-class culture it cannot serve to reduce class inequality while the core of citizenship comprises only civil rights. The significance of social rights in citizenship is precisely that they tend to remove the illegitimate inequalities from the class system, and in doing so perform a key integrative function. This argument has been extensively treated in previous chapters and there is no need to repeat it here. What should be noted, though, is that the material civilization on which the development of citizenship draws and which it defends is one in which mass production in the economy plays a central role. According to Marshall mass production is made feasible precisely because of the nature of the modern class system which resulted from the destruction of distinct class cultures in the eighteenth century through the effects of civil rights. The various threads of this general argument were brought together by Marshall a few years before he published them in *Citizenship and Social Class*. In 'Work and Wealth' Marshall (1945: 216–7) says that:

> There has been going on, especially in the last fifty years or so, a steady fusion of class civilizations into a single national civilization . . . There was a time when the culture of each class was, as it were, a unique species . . . Mass production destroyed this isolation . . . There has been a progressive equalization of the quality of material culture so that, even though great differences remain between the top and the bottom, they are variations on a single theme and are linked in a continuous scale . . . [Among other things it follows that] as higher quality goods move down the social scale, so hands reach up towards them from below and voices are lifted demanding a speedier rise in the standard of living.

The implication of this argument is that as a mass material culture emerges all classes can be seen to exist on a more or less common scale and the lower-class struggle to improve its situation is therefore an aspect of development within a material civilization it shares with other classes. Thus social integration is attained through economic well-being within a societally uniform standard. This is a distinctive approach which moves away from the idea of a normative acceptance of institutions and practices to a practical expectation that the system will satisfy the material interests of all sections of the population and not simply the powerful (Lipset 1969: 77; Poggi 1978: 132–4). Marshall's account of the integrative capacity of citizenship is particularly interesting because, unlike most accounts of the integrative consequences of citizenship, it focuses on material culture and implicitly gives a diminished role to political citizenship as an integrative force.

It can be seen that Marshall's account of integration has three distinct components. First, citizenship as civil rights creates a class system in which distinct class cultures diminish. Secondly, citizenship, especially through social rights, removes the significance of class inequalities. Third, mass production creates a common material civilization in which the demand for the expansion of citizenship is enhanced. Thus Marshall's theory of integration only partly depends on the concept of citizenship, and he belongs to a tradition which does not emphasize normative integration but integration based on the satisfaction of material interests.

The real limitation of Marshall's treatment of civilization is not that it is normative or vague. Rather it is that a concept of material civilization or culture is simply too narrow to adequately treat the question of social integration. Marshall is to be applauded, certainly, for introducing the mundane necessities of practical well-being into the notion of 'civilization'; although paradoxically this usage is less novel for his generation than it is for us today. The Victorians who were Marshall's teachers and intellectual influences were aware that the exclusion of the working class from civilization constituted its greatest threat, a threat that could only be averted by opening civilization to the working class and including them in it. For the cultural incorporation of the working class it was required that their economic improvement be accepted. In this sense the material component of civilization was well understood by Marshall and his generation.

Marshall's general conceptualization of integration has clear limitations however, for it assumes that core assumptions of a civilization or culture are more or less stable and that integration is a process of historical expansion through incorporation of different groups within a common national community. It is for this reason that Marshall's formulation does not readily adapt to considerations of the integration or assimilation of culturally distinct migrant groups into a host societal community. This latter case raises a quite different question of 'common civilization' from the one treated by Marshall.

Bryan Turner (1986: 46) correctly takes Marshall to task for taking the British nation-state for granted, but in the context outlined here the problem is rather deeper. Talcott Parsons' (1965) concern with 'common values' in the definition of citizenship has a real basis in so far as his discussion of negro integration into American society must lead to the recognition that integration cannot simply be achieved by the negro acceptance of American mores, but requires the alteration of such norms and values in the American ethos as would permit the inclusion of negros with white Americans in a common and significantly new 'civilization'. Marshall (1969: 147–51) approaches this realization in his discussion of the Black Power movement in America during the 1960s, when he says that 'Black power does not seek admission into American society as it is. The goal is a new kind of society, truly multi-racial' (Marshall 1969: 150). But there is no reformulation of his general account of social integration or of citizenship.

When Marshall (1975: 207) describes the 'lack of a capacity to feel or act as a full and equal member of the community' in terms of 'a dislike of being involved with officials . . . ignorance of what one's rights really are and of the procedure to be followed in presenting them' and so on, he is referring to a situation which cannot be understood simply through his concept of a common material civilization based upon mass production.

iv

There is another aspect of Marshall's account of social integration which other treatments frequently ignore. It has been shown in previous chapters that Marshall (1950: 114, 122) regards the contradiction between citizenship rights and class inequality or the market system as unending. The process upon which integration is based is that of equalization within a material culture as the basis of a common civilization which renders class inequalities irrelevant.

This will not be a secure source of integration if conflict between citizenship and social class is chronic. For Marshall, then, social integration is never final or finally achieved. It is for this reason that Lockwood suggests that the emphasis on the integrative aspect of citizenship is an unnecessary exaggeration and distortion of Marshall's position.

Marshall's argument of how the modern development of the status of citizenship forms the basis of an abatement and institutionalization of class conflict 'is now part of the sociological tradition' (Lockwood 1974: 366). But this aspect of Marshall's account of citizenship is not the whole. Indeed, Lockwood (1974: 366) goes on to warn that 'this picture has perhaps been overdrawn and Marshall's statement that "in the twentieth century citizenship and the capitalist class system have been at war" has not been sufficiently well understood as indicating a source of inherent and continuing tension in these societies'. Since Lockwood wrote these words commentators have extensively highlighted what earlier readers of Marshall tended to ignore. Bryan Turner (1986: 37) in particular bases his own analysis of capitalist development on an interpretation of Marshall which emphasizes that 'there is no inbuilt assumption [in Marshall] about either equilibrium or about social consensus; indeed it is assumed that conflict is the normal state of affairs in a competitive and market-dominated society'.

It is true that from his early writing (1938) to the most recent (1981a) Marshall recognizes that there is unavoidable and continuing disagreement, friction and conflict in capitalist-democratic societies. More particularly, his understanding of the integration achieved through the development of citizenship is of an integration which is not nor could be a final and accomplished fact, but part of a process which is never complete and always uneasy. In other words, and it is very important to emphasize this point, Marshall's account of social integration is one which insists that integration is ever problematic. This is so because, as Marshall makes amply clear in *Citizenship and Social Class*, and as Lockwood and others have reminded us, the egalitarian consequences of the development of citizenship status have unavoidable limitations and class differences cannot be entirely eliminated by them, and, secondly, the basic contradiction between citizenship rights and market forces has not been and cannot be eliminated.

In a later paper Marshall (1961) treats the rise and decline of the welfare state in Britain from the 1940s to the 1960s as a case study in order to examine the uneasy attainment of social and political integration. In particular Marshall (1961: 280) is interested in the way in which consensus about particular social institutions can enhance a general integrative process, and also in historical variation in the strength of consensus and the extent of integration. Although Marshall fails to explicitly draw general conclusions he says that the social integration achieved by the welfare state resting on the Beveridge Report and the National Health Service had as its preconditions certain 'social and economic conditions which had emerged from the period of common effort and common endurance during the war' (Marshall 1961: 293). The rise of the 'affluent society' by the mid-1950s, together with an inflationary economy, provided another set of social and economic conditions which Marshall (1961: 294–5) says undermined the principles of the welfare state.

The conclusions of this discussion are entirely in keeping with Marshall's earlier cautions about the relatively precarious nature of the attainment of integration, especially through the development of citizenship. But the limitations of Marshall's approach are more evident here than they are in *Citizenship and Social Class*. It is clear in Marshall's (1961) later discussion of the welfare state that the social and economic conditions through which the sources of integration are efficacious have an existence which is quite independent of the institutions of citizenship. As these change so the possibilities for social integration also change. This is not a remarkable observation in itself, but it highlights an aspect of Marshall's general account which is almost wholly overlooked.

Marshall (1950) argues that the development of citizenship provides an equal status which in reducing the social significance of class inequality tends to reduce class conflict and tension and thereby enhances social integration. At the same time Marshall insists that the contradiction between citizenship and class is fundamental and irresolvable, and therefore that integration is never complete and class conflict and tension always possible. If class inequality is abated by citizenship, the question remains of what is the source of emergent tension and conflict. Marshall in fact cannot answer this because he has no account of the dynamics of class and distributional relationships independent of his account of citizenship. Ralf Dahrendorf (1959) pointed to this fundamental limitation of Marshall's account some time ago, but it has been subsequently ignored.

Dahrendorf (1959: 107–8) shows that because Marshall leaves 'entirely untouched . . . the problem of power or authority and its social distribution' the conflicts and tensions he refers to are 'essentially random phenomena'. Dahrendorf continues by saying that this is because Marshall 'excludes the problem of power and authority from social analysis, [and he therefore] abandons the possibility to trace social conflicts back to structural conditions'. One does not have to subscribe to Dahrendorf's own position on class to recognize the pertinence of his comments on Marshall. What is being argued here is that while Marshall understands that integration can never be final, his recognition of the fact is entirely anomalous in terms of his account of the role of citizenship in the integrative process.

7

Social Movements in Citizenship

It was shown in the last two chapters that while the integrative role cannot be ignored, it far from exhausts all the possible consequences of citizenship. By designating membership in a national community citizenship also defines non-membership. Those excluded from the citizenship status may find it necessary to resort to force in attempting to attain inclusion and the advantages inclusion provides. Thus citizenship may be a source of conflict as well as integration. But conflict is too narrow a category to cover the non-integrative aspects of citizenship. The obverse of integration is not disintegration nor even conflict but movement. The concept of social movement brought to a discussion of citizenship raises a number of interesting questions.

At the most general level social movements can be said to arise out of collective social action. Social movements, unlike political movements, are not directed to capturing political power but express the aspirations – interests, values and norms – of social collectivities. Social movement is therefore associated with social change through modification of the expectations and mores which influence social relationships. As a means of cultural change social movements redefine what social participation may consist of.

While social movements may advance the development of citizenship, citizenship rights facilitate the emergence of social movements. Given the two-way relationship between citizenship and social movement indicated here it is appropriate to ask whether a framework which poses the questions concerning citizenship in terms of social class, which has been taken for granted throughout the discussion so far, as opposed to social movement, is entirely appropriate. These are the issues to be treated in this chapter.

i

There is a comprehensive involvement of various civil rights in the formation and performance of social movements. As a form of collective action drawing upon persons of diverse background social movements are composed of members legally and socially constituted as private individuals. Persons are linked in social movements through a shared self-consciousness of purpose which is supported by the freedoms of association and expression. Thus it is with some reason that Marshall (1969: 145) is able to say that civil rights 'might usefully be regarded as a form of power' because they provide the persons who have them with 'the capacity for successful action'. The significance for the emergence of social movements is summarized in Marshall's (1969: 142) statement that 'civil rights, though vested in individuals, are used to create groups, associations, corporations and movements of every kind'.

The conditions for the formation of social movements and other social collectivities cannot be reduced to civil rights, of course. Social organization in this sense requires members who can draw upon material and interactional resources, in addition to norms and rights. Yet normative permissibility plays a role which is too easily underrated. Ralf Dahrendorf (1959: 186) goes so far as to say that in the absence of the right to association the other conditions are unlikely to produce social organization or movement. However, the suppression of movements through the absence of civil rights and even their repression through police force does not necessarily mean that their prospects are impossible.

In 'Reflections on Power' Marshall (1969: 145–51) argues that in the effective absence of civil rights, social movement itself can be an alternative source of power in providing a capacity for successful action. Marshall refers to the Black Power Movement and the Student Movement in particular, but the point is applicable to social movements in general. What is not available as a right may be achieved through usurpation and the mobilization of numbers. Discussion here leads to the apparently paradoxical conclusion that social movements both contribute to and are facilitated by citizenship. As we shall see, different conceptions of social movement apply to these different possibilities.

ii

The development of citizenship has two analytically distinct aspects: there is the inclusion of new categories of persons into existing citizenship rights, and there is the advent of new types of rights in citizenship, the creation of new components or elements of citizenship. These different processes may historically occur together, although they need not. While an expansion of the numbers of citizens seldom in itself leads to changes in the structure of citizenship, the creation of new types of citizenship rights frequently inducts previously excluded sections of the population into a national community, as when the nineteenth century creation of political citizenship brought sections of the working class into the operations of European societies for the first time. It is important to stress that these distinct aspects of the development of citizenship entail rather different sociological processes and draw upon different aspects, indeed, different understandings, of social movement.

The inclusion of migrants into a host-nation's citizenship structure is the most obvious case of the development of citizenship through increases in the numbers of persons meeting existing criteria of membership rather than through the advent of new rights as components or elements of citizenship. An interesting account of the processes involved in increasing citizen participation is outlined by Talcott Parsons (1965) in his paper 'Full Citizenship for the Negro American?'.

Parsons (1965: 263) argues that the inclusion of previously excluded groups into full membership of society can be analysed in terms of a model drawn from the 'supply and demand' paradigm of economics. Demands for inclusion can come both from the excluded group and from elements of the 'included' population. The 'supply' component for the excluded groups refers to their qualifications for membership, which is a matter of what Parsons calls their 'cultural and social structures'. The receiving community, at the same time, must 'supply' a pattern of citizenship rights which can be exercised by those seeking membership in the host community.

The economic analogy outlined by Parsons is most apt when the process of inclusion is implemented through an exchange in which those who can supply the appropriate social and cultural qualifications are on that basis given the opportunity to exercise the citizenship rights associated with them. Parsons (1965: 264) suggests that the economic analogy is indeed appropriate in the majority of cases of new immigration when he says that 'much of the actual process [of inclusion] often occurs inconspicuously without much of a movement'. In the case of the inclusion of negro Americans, however, whose immigration significantly pre-dates their endeavours for inclusion in American society, Parsons immediately adds that 'as expression and implementation of demand in the present sense, the relevant *movements* have a very important place in our analysis'. Although Parsons seems not to realize it, the relevance of movements to the analysis of the inclusion of new groups in established citizenship processes indicates that the economic model has to be replaced by an explicitly political model, which Parsons goes on to briefly outline without in fact acknowledging or recognizing that a paradigm shift has taken place.

Movements for inclusion are significant because of both the time at which they gain importance and the consequences they have for the development of citizenship. Parsons (1965: 264) says that:

> Such movements tend to gather strength as the strain of conflict between the normative requirements for inclusion and the factual limitations on it are translated into pressures to act. Movements, however, not only express strain in this sense, but 'stir things up' further. Thus, their consequences are often relatively unpredictable.

The second point mentioned here, that movements are not only consequences of social situations but also creators of them, is crucial to the definition of social movements as agents (rather than merely products) of social change. In particular Parsons is suggesting that the outcome of a mobilized pressure for inclusion cannot itself necessarily achieve what it seeks. By setting in train events and creating circumstances which would include the participation of new actors in the situation, social movements will influence the outcome of processes they join in a way which is not predictable and certainly may not lead to the inclusion of the groups whose interests they purport to advance.

This point is very important because it reminds us that citizenship participation and rights are not necessarily achieved by struggle and movement. For this reason the inclusion of the concept 'social movement' in the argument about the secondary rights of citizenship, outlined in Chapter 2 above, avoids the conclusion so often associated with it, namely that there is a 'logic of citizenship' such that once civil rights are achieved other types of citizenship rights emerge in due course. If the use of civil rights to achieve industrial or political rights, say, is mediated through social movement, the consolidation of these latter rights as citizenship rights is a consequence of the success of movement rather than a logical entailment of other rights in civil rights, and is therefore always precarious and contingent.

Social movements become most crucial in the struggle for the expansion of citizenship at the time the resolve of those opposing increased participation is at its highest. Implicit in Parsons' discussion above, but not adequately brought out in it, is the notion that the more exclusion itself is felt to be the principal factor separating the excluded group from the community as a whole the more intense will be an excluded group's demand for inclusion and the more likely it will be to attract support. If the chief source of this feeling is the excluded group's commitment to the prevailing values of the host community rather than a symmetry of cultural and social structures between the two, then inclusion is likely to be resisted by key elements in the existing community of participation, and the aspirant group's endeavours frustrated. The social movement responds to this situation by intensifying its efforts.

In this account the defining characteristic of social movement is its capacity to mobilize resources, and the cultural definition of both the structure of citizenship and, therefore, the host community on the one hand, and the excluded or aspirant group on the other, are taken for granted or assumed to be given. An aspect of the American Civil Rights movement in particular, however, is that it not only served to mobilize resources for social change by insinuating negros into locations in the social structure previously denied them, but also culturally redefined Blacks in a manner which in turn led to a reappraisal and redefinition of American institutions in general. Parsons surprisingly fails to include an apprehension of such developments in his basic categories.

Two quite different conceptions of social movement have been indicated here. Parsons' discussion parallels the approach to social movements which sees them as particular instances of collective behaviour primarily oriented to the mobilization of social resources for the purposes of interested action which has largely organizational consequences for the society in which they occur. A quite different understanding of social movements regards them principally as the basis and source of cultural transformation in society, as being responsible for changes in the way that society, its members and their relationships, are defined and understood. Alain Touraine (1977: 315), who is particularly associated with this second understanding of social movement, says that 'a social movement is constantly occupied with challenging the social definition of roles, the functioning of the political arena, and the social order'. From this perspective social movements are a form of action which transform historically given cultural patterns. It is in this sense that the nineteenth-century English labour movement, for instance, provides an excellent example of social movement as its emergence not only destroyed the liberal understanding of human nature but among other things also led to an entirely new conception of society and its animus (Macpherson 1973: 200–2).

iii

The relevance of the conception of social movement as a mediator of cultural change to the question of citizenship has recently been emphasized by Bryan Turner. Turner (1986: 92) argues that as the redefinition of society and therefore social membership is the intention or outcome of social movements, social movements are 'inevitably movements about the rights of citizenship'. In this way it is possible to describe the historical development of citizenship not only in terms of its elements or components, as Marshall had done, but also in terms of the consequences for the definition of social membership of successive occurrences, incidents or episodes of social movement. Turner (1986: 97–8) says that there have been four such 'waves' in the development of modern citizenship: the first had the consequence of removing property from the definition of the citizen; the second removed sex; the third wave redefined the significance of age and kinship ties in the family for citizenship rights; and a fourth wave, according to Turner, is currently expanding citizenship by ascribing rights to nature and the environment.

This scheme is inventive and stimulating, certainly, but in presenting a post-hoc summary of historical changes rather than a conceptual classification of types its role in understanding the development of citizenship is not clear, and somewhat limited. Although it refers to historical developments Turner's scheme fails to adequately reflect the history of social movements. For instance, the feminist movement is given representation in his second wave only although its impact on social participation has been and continues to be more extensive than Turner's scheme suggests. Secondly, Turner's scheme can neither replace nor usefully supplement Marshall's distinction between civil, political and social rights in the development of citizenship. This is principally because

Turner's scheme conflates and collapses the question of the participation of groups in citizenship with that of the different rights of citizenship in which they participate.

Perhaps the most telling limitation of Turner's approach is that it assumes that changing cultural definitions of social membership will necessarily correspond with the activity and influence of different social movements. Leaving this question aside, Turner fails to appreciate that social movements as he understands them could at best provide no more than the preconditions for an increased participation in citizenship through change in the culturally per-ceived criteria of social membership. The creation of new elements of citizenship, such as political or social rights, is in practice realized through a set of processes which cannot be reduced to a redefinition of social membership but must also include not only social movement as resource mobilization, but more crucially political, bureaucratic, administrative and legal practices which may be at best only remotely associated with social movement and are indeed likely to be quite unconnected with such a phenomenon.

Turner introduces his account of the development of citizenship through 'waves' of movement and cultural redefinition in the context of a general dissatisfaction with the association of citizen-ship and social class, and a preference for social movement over class as a more valid category for understanding the development of citizenship. Turner (1986: 88) insists that the argument about the development of citizenship in terms of social class is inherently problematic because of two factors. He questions the validity of class theory and analysis in general, and he doubts the relevance of the class concept for an understanding of the development of citizenship. Turner (1986: 88–9) goes on to argue that much of the struggle for greater participation in society involves social move-ments rather than social classes, and that these movements cannot be reduced to their class composition.

There is no need to dispute that it is possible and frequently useful to recognize the relevance of social movements to the development of citizenship, as indicated earlier in this chapter. The women's movement in particular has not only been instrumental in increasing the numbers of persons who can count as full members of society, but has also influenced the nature of the rights exercised in social participation. It is not entirely clear, though, why this fact undermines the validity of the concept 'social class' in the discussion of citizenship, among other things, as a number of writers, including

Turner, assume. What has to be considered is the relationship between social movement and social class.

Some of these matters are elaborated by Claus Offe (1985) in an important contribution to the discussion of social movements. According to Offe (1985: 835) the pattern of social and political conflict expressed in the new social movements is 'the polar opposite of the model of class conflict'. This is because, firstly, social-movement conflict is conducted by an 'alliance that consists, in varying proportions, of elements coming from different classes and "nonclasses" '. The imputation here is that class conflict, on the other hand, is staged by one class against another. Also social-movement demands are either more or less inclusive than class-specific demands, that is, they tend to be either strongly universal-istic or highly particularistic. It will be shown that these points are insufficient to distinguish social-movement conflict from class conflict, and that they fail to demonstrate that the two are polar opposites.

In making the first point above Offe seems not to appreciate the role of social alliance in class conflict. It was indicated a number of times in Chapter 3 that in its struggle for citizenship rights the working class has always relied on alliances with others, including elements of other classes and non-class social forces such as victorious foreign armies. The idea that the agents of class conflict are something other than class alliances is in fact difficult to discover in the relevant literature. In Marx's historical writings, for instance, and in the *Communist Manifesto*, and in practically all of Lenin's relevant work, class conflict is always treated as conflict between sets of alliances. The composition of these alliances is held to be different in different social settings and at different stages of class struggle, but typically in these works the working-class struggles in alliance with sections of the ruling and middle classes and peasantry; and, for its part, the ruling class allies itself with sections of the middle class and the lumpenproleteriat.

Although neither Offe nor Turner mention it explicitly, others doubtful about the political relevance of the class concept argue that if class is an aspect of social structure, then classes as such cannot act, and therefore cannot struggle, form alliances, and so on. Again, such views are based on a limited appreciation of the class concept. Max Weber's (1921: 930–2) discussion of class conflict, for instance, emphasizes the fact that the actors in class struggle can never be classes as such, because the basis of all class action is in the formation of a 'group' drawn from but not equivalent to the aggregation of common class situations. Although Weber intended this formulation to be an alternative to the Marxist treatment of class conflict it is in this regard similar to it. Marx distinguishes between class as an objective circumstance (class-in-itself) and class as a political force based on associations formed through recognition of a consciousness of shared conditions (class-for-itself). The general point here is that for Marx, as for Weber, actors in class struggle are not classes as elements of social structure but are social groups formed on a basis of common class-identity. We will return to this point in the following section.

Turner (1986: 88) does not wholly reject the use of the class concept for social analysis when he acknowledges that social movements 'have a complex class composition'. This is a view which Offe also accepts. He describes the social-structural composition of the new social movements as being significantly 'rooted in major segments of the new middle class' (Offe 1985: 832). This is important in the present context because a leading characteristic of the new middle class is that while it is 'class-aware' it is not 'class-conscious'. This means that the demands shaped by the core of the new social movements 'are highly class-*un*specific, dispersed, and either "universalistic" in nature (e.g. environmental, peace, and civil rights concerns) *or* highly concentrated on particular groups (defined, for instance, by locality, age, or their being affected situationally by certain practices, laws, or institutions of the state)' (Offe 1985: 833). To insist in this context that class conflict be characterized by 'class' demands and that social-movement conflict be characterized by non-class demands thus becomes entirely arbitrary when it is acknowledged that the social structure of each can readily be treated in terms of their social class composition. Offe shows that the nature of the demands made in conflict situations will vary with the class-basis of the dominant faction of the social alliances involved. That is all.

The problem here is that Offe claims to make a case about types of conflict but presents an argument about the demands and self-images of participants. Indeed, a large element of what distinguishes 'class conflict' from 'social-movement conflict' is precisely the self-identity of the participants. It is not useful to describe all social movements as (alliances of) class agents, but the discussion above demonstrates that it is sensible to describe the class agents in social struggle as movements. In real terms, then, whether the struggle for citizenship is described in terms of class or movement principally depends on how the participants define themselves. A strong analytic distinction between them is entirely question begging.

iv

The identity of social groups or movements may be based on class loyalty or on religious, ethnic, national, sexual, or some other attachment. In this sense 'class' and 'ethnicity', for example, can be said to be in competition with each other. If the predominant type of social identity in any given situation takes a non-class form it would follow that 'class' has been displaced by some other social force. But, as we saw above, such a statement ignores a dimension of the class concept which is in fact prior to class identity.

Unlike Turner, Alain Touraine (1977) insists that classes and social movements are quite different types of phenomena which bear a non-contradictory relationship with each other. In a characterization interestingly similar to Marx's distinction between a class-in-itself and a class-for-itself Touraine characterizes classes as social situations or conditions and social movements as collective actors. While collective action is not possible for classes as situations or conditions, the membership of social movements is drawn from persons with clear and distinct class backgrounds, although social movements need not be defined in terms of the social class composition of their membership (Touraine 1977: 310–18).

In his analysis of citizenship Marshall (1950) is concerned with the consequences of the expansion of rights on class structure as an objective situation in something of the manner indicated by Touraine, and also on the level of class resentment. Class resentment relates to the propensity of conflict rather than to the identity to which one subscribes when engaged in conflict, or any other form of group involvement and membership. As we saw in an earlier chapter, Marshall has very little to say about the role of class or social-movement conflict in the expansion of citizenship. Turner's complaint against a discussion of the expansion of citizenship in terms of social class is encouraged by the view that in extending the scope of participation in society the growth of citizenship has tended to undermine the significance of class in the social structure.

The notion that class is no longer a useful category for measuring social structure strongly encourages the more general view that class is a less valid notion for understanding the expansion of citizenship than social movement. A strong caution against this conclusion is warranted because it is not at all clear that even the full development of social citizenship negates social class. It was shown in Chapter 4 that while the development of social participation may indeed diminish class resentment, it cannot dismantle the pattern of class inequality in the social structure. The self-identity of the movements which seek to modify the patterns of both social participation and social inequality are inevitably different at different times, but the conclusions to be drawn from this fact should not be exaggerated. It must be added that the suggestion that 'class conflict' has been displaced from the Western political arena by 'social-movement conflict' is both premature and misleading (Bottomore 1984; Wood 1986).

The real strength of Marshall's treatment of the development of citizenship, which may be lost if the focus of analysis is simply on those who struggle for increased participation, is that it leads to a serious consideration of the consequences of citizenship rights and their institutional bases on social organization and social structure. The concept of class is crucial for such an analysis, a fact Marshall appreciated through a very strong sense of the concrete historical reality of capitalism as a social system.

8

Conclusion: The State and Citizenship

The interest of Marshall's contribution to the theory of citizenship is that it places the conventional question of participation in political community in the important context of social institutions and processes. The limitation of Marshall's approach, some aspects of which have been highlighted in previous chapters, could not detract from its significance in raising crucial questions concerning the connections and interactions between political arrangements and social structure.

While there is now an extensive (although less then coherent) literature which attempts to build on, correct and extend Marshall's treatment of citizenship and social class there is still nothing which could be described as a *theory* of citizenship. The background to this default can be indicated in the failure of alternative statements of Marshall's position to add together in the production of an account which treats the salient issues from a single explanatory viewpoint. For instance, Anthony Giddens (1982) complains that Marshall fails to appreciate the role of struggle in the development of social citizenship, although others, including Bryan Turner (1986), claim Marshall as the source of this insight. In either case, the insertion of the concept of 'struggle' in an account of the historic expansion of social participation may lead away from the idea that the trend of development is evolutionary and irreversible, which with some justification Giddens understands to be Marshall's position. But at the same time this approach totally fails to appreciate both that struggle may also lead to repression rather than to increased rights, and that citizenship rights may be extended for reasons only partly if at all associated with social struggle; matters which were treated in Chapters 3 and 5.

It was shown in Chapter 2 that Marshall fails to adequately

consider the relationship between the different elements of citizenship. Through the concept of secondary rights he proposes a treatment of their serial development, and he also shows how civil rights on the one hand and political and social rights on the other bear a different – indeed opposite – relationship with market relations and class inequality. What he fails to treat, though, is the means through which the distinct sets of rights function together as components of a unified citizenship. Given that the individual sets of rights tend to pull in different directions this is ultimately a question about the state's promotion and safeguard of citizenship rights. Marshall takes the state for granted and fails to reflect upon its significance for the development of citizenship. He tends to share this inclination with his critics. But the role of the state in the development of citizenship is crucial; and any theory of political and social participation and rights must acknowledge and build on the fact.

In an extension of Marshall's analysis of the institutionalization of class conflict to non-British and non-democratic cases Michael Mann (1987) clearly highlights the crucial explanatory significance of the state in determining the processes of social participation and the formation of citizenship rights. But because the focus of this account is ruling-class *strategies* it dissolves the institutional distinction between social interest and state organization; 'ruling class' for Mann (1987: 340) means 'a combination of the dominant economic class and the political and military rulers'. In addition, because Mann is concerned to indicate particular historical examples he does not outline general formulations.

The first general thing of relevance concerning the state is that in creating and enforcing the rules or laws to which all social entities are subject it constitutes the principal expression of political power in national societies. Secondly, the state itself can be described as a network of power relations between the distinct organizations involved in the promulgation, interpretation, application and enforcement of law. The third thing, which appears to be in tension with the other two, is that in a real sense the state's power is not independent or autonomous. No state can continue to rule in the absence of firm support from significant social classes and groups. It is this factor which permits accounts such as Mann's mentioned above to treat the concept 'ruling class' as an amalgam of economically dominant class and political elite.

In the historical development of the capitalist state the

coincidence of interest of state organization and economically dominant class fixed the question of citizenship fairly predictably. Although they offer different accounts of it both Marx and Weber agree that the political state enhances the capitalist class. 'Out of this alliance of the state with capital', says Max Weber (1925: 337), 'arose the national citizen class, the bourgeoisie in the modern sense of the word'. The obvious and manifest nexus of dominant class and state remains unproblematic while the relations between the dominant and subordinate social classes are overlain with status relations of social acceptance and deference. In the advance of capitalist relations, however, dominant classes abrogate their responsibility towards subordinate classes and initiate a political mobilization in which the state becomes a key agent.

The conventional argument is that as the organized labour movement gained strength it fought for and won rights and conditions from both the state and the bourgeoisie. It has been shown in other chapters that this account requires substantial qualification. It was noted above that the state cannot rule in the absence of support from significant social classes and groups. While all forms of political state are limited by the requirement that they enjoy the support of their subjects, this limitation is not absolute as states are able to influence the nature of their appeal and also the orientation of their subjects.

Faced with pressures for change states have three options. They may ignore them, they may accede to them, or they may repress the groups demanding them. The choice taken can be explained in terms of whether it enhances or detracts from the state's capacity to rule, and in the context of what has been said this amounts to the question of whether it will consolidate or alienate support from the state's social base. Such calculations will alway be contingent, so that demands ignored at one time will meet forceful repression at another, only to be agreed to at a later stage, and possibly cancelled at some future time, all depending on the (changing) balance of social forces and the state's calculus of its security. On the basis of this reasoning it is also possible that changes may be initiated by the state in order to avert a situation it foresees or to take advantage of an opportunity it recognizes. In any event it is crucial to accept that no matter how intense the struggle for citizenship rights, it is the state which ultimately grants them, and it may choose to do so even in the absence of such a struggle. It has to be added that the denial of rights and not simply their extension may at certain times and in certain contexts also enhance a state's rule.

This type of account does not undermine Marshall's treatment of the sequential development of the civil, political and social elements of citizenship in Britain, but it does raise questions about the conditions of their emergence which his approach neglects. More importantly the approach briefly and inadequately indicated here allows us to fit into a single framework the various criticisms of Marshall's discussion and those of his critics which were spelled out in the preceding chapters. And perhaps even more important, this approach clears the way for an understanding of the loss of rights as well as their positive development, which is the more relevant consideration for the decades ahead.

Bibliography

Bendix, R. (1964) 'Transformations of western European societies since the eighteenth century.' In his *Nation-Building and Citizenship*. New York, John Wiley and Sons.

Bendix, R. (1974) *Work and Authority in Industry*, Berkeley, University of California Press.

Bottomore, T. (1984) 'The political role of the working class in western Europe'. In his *Sociology and Socialism*, Brighton, Wheatsheaf Books.

Briggs, A. (1961) [1967] 'The welfare state in historical perspective'. In C. I. Schottland (ed.) *The Welfare State: Selected Essays*, New York, Harper and Row.

Brown, H. P. (1983) *The Origins of Trade Union Power*, Oxford, Oxford University Press.

Castles, F. (1978) *The Social Democratic Image of Society*, London, Routledge and Kegan Paul.

Clarke, S. (1982) *Marx, Marginalism and Modern Sociology*, London, Macmillan.

Cole, G. D. H. and Postgate, R. (1946) *The Common People, 1746–1946*, London, Methuen.

Dahrendorf, R. (1959) *Class and Class Conflict in Industrial Society*, London, Routledge and Kegan Paul.

Dahrendorf, R. (1969) *Society and Democracy in Germany*, New York, Doubleday.

Dahrendorf, R. (1973) 'A personal vote of thanks'. *British Journal of Sociology*, 24(4).

Dawson, W. H. (1890) *Bismarck and State Socialism: An Exposition of Social and Economic Legislation in Germany since 1870*, London, Swan and Sonnenschein.

Durkheim, E. (1893) [1964] *The Division of Labor in Society*, New York, Free Press.

Gallie, D. (1983) *Social Inequality and Class Radicalism in France and Britain*, London, Cambridge University Press.

Giddens, A. (1979) *Central Problems in Social Theory*, London, Macmillan.

Giddens, A. (1982) 'Class division, class conflict and citizenship rights'. In his *Profiles and Critiques and Social Theory*, London, Macmillan.

Goldthorpe, J. (1974) 'Social inequality and social integration in modern Britain'. In D. Wedderburn (ed.) *Poverty, Inequality and Class Structure*, London, Cambridge University Press.

Goldthorpe, J. (1978) 'The current inflation: towards a sociological account'. In F. Hirsch and J. Goldthorpe (eds) *The Political Economy of Inflation*, London, Martin Robertson.

Greaves, H. R. G. (1966) *The Foundations of Political Theory*, London, Bell and Sons. 2nd edition.

Hacker, A. (1965) 'Power to do what?' In I. L. Horowitz (ed.) *The New Sociology*, New York, Oxford University Press.

Halsey, A. H. (1984) 'T. H. Marshall: past and present'. *Sociology*, 18(1).

Hay, J. R. (1978) 'Employers' attitudes to social policy and the concept of "social control", 1900–1920'. In P. Thane (ed.) *The Origins of British Social Policy*, London, Croom Helm.

Heclo, H. (1974) *Modern Social Politics in Britain and Sweden*, New Haven, Yale University Press.

Hindess, B. (1987) *Freedom, Equality and the Market*, London, Tavistock.

Hobhouse, L. T. (1928) *Social Evolution and Political Theory*, New York, Columbia University Press.

Janowitz, M. (1980) 'Observations on the sociology of citizenship: obligations and rights'. *Social Forces*, 59(1).

Kalecki, M. (1943) [1972] 'Political aspects of full employment'. In E. K. Hunt and J. G. Schwartz (eds) *A Critique of Economic Theory*, Harmondsworth, Penguin.

Klein, R. (1983) *The Politics of the National Health Service*, London, Longman.

Korpi, W. (1978) *The Working Class in Welfare Capitalism*, London, Routledge and Kegan Paul.

le Grand, J. (1982) *The Strategy of Equality*, London, Allen and Unwin.

Lenin, V. I. (1916) [1964] 'Imperialism and the split in socialism'. In his *Collected Works*, volume 23. London, Lawrence and Wishart.

Lindblom, C. (1977) *Politics and Markets*, New York, Basic Books.

Lipset, S. M. (1964) Introduction. In Marshall 1973.

Lipset, S. M. (1969) *Political Man*, London, Heinemann.

Lockwood, D. (1964) 'Social integration and system integration'. In G. K. Zollschan and W. Hirsch (eds) *Explorations in Social Change*, Boston, Houghton-Mifflin.

Lockwood, D. (1974) 'For T. H. Marshall'. *Sociology*, 8(3).

Macpherson, C. B. (1973) *Democratic Theory*, Oxford, Oxford University Press.

Macpherson, C. B. (1985) 'Problems of human rights in the late twentieth century'. In his *The Rise and Fall of Economic Justice and Other Essays*. Oxford, Oxford University Press.

MacRae, D. G. (1974) *Weber*, London, Fontana/Collins.

Mann, M. (1987) 'Ruling class strategies and citizenship'. *Sociology*, 21(3).

Marshall, T. H. (1934) 'Social class – a preliminary analysis'. Pagination as in Marshall 1950a.

Marshall, T. H. (1938) 'The nature of class conflict'. Pagination as in Marshall 1973.

Marshall, T. H. (1945) 'Work and wealth'. Pagination as in Marshall 1973.

Marshall, T. H. (1950) 'Citizenship and social class'. Pagination as in Marshall 1973.

Marshall, T. H. (1950a) *Citizenship and Social Class and Other Essays*, Cambridge, Cambridge University Press.

Marshall, T. H. (1953) 'Social selection in the welfare state'. Pagination as in Marshall 1973.

Marshall, T. H. (1954) 'A note on "status" '. Pagination as in Marshall 1973.

Marshall, T. H. (1956) 'Changes in social stratification in the twentieth century'. Pagination as in Marshall 1973.

Marshall, T. H. (1961) 'The welfare state – a comparative study'. Pagination as in Marshall 1973.

Marshall, T. H. (1961a) 'The welfare state and the affluent society'. Pagination as in Marshall 1973.

Marshall, T. H. (1963) *Sociology at the Crossroads and Other Essays*, London, Heinemann.

Marshall, T. H. (1969) 'Reflections on power'. Pagination as in Marshall 1981.

Marshall, T. H. (1972) 'Value problems of welfare-capitalism'. Pagination as in Marshall 1981.

Marshall, T. H. (1973) *Class, Citizenship and Social Development*, Westport, Connecticut, Greenwood Press. [First published in 1964, this differs from Marshall 1963 only through the addition of an introduction by S. M. Lipset.]

Marshall, T. H. (1975) *Social Policy in the Twentieth Century*, London, Hutchinson. 4th edition.

Marshall, T. H. (1981) *The Right to Welfare and Other Essays*, London, Heinemann.

Marshall, T. H. (1981a) 'Afterthought'. Pagination as in Marshall 1981.

Marx, K. (1843) [1975] 'On the Jewish question'. In his *Early Writings*, Harmondsworth, Penguin.

Middlemas, K. (1979) *Politics in Industrial Society*, London, Andre Deutsch.

Miliband, R. (1984) *Capitalist Democracy in Britain*, Oxford, Oxford University Press.

Milward, A. S. (1984) *The Economic Effects of the Two World Wars on Britain*, London, Macmillan. 2nd edition.

Moore, B. (1969) *Social Origins of Dictatorship and Democracy*, Harmondsworth, Penguin.

Moorhouse, H. F. (1973) 'The political incorporation of the British working class: an interpretation'. *Sociology*, 7(3).

Offe, C. (1985) 'New social movements: challenging the boundaries of institutional politics'. *Social Research*, 52(4).

Ossowski, S. (1963) *Class Structure in the Social Consciousness*, London, Routledge and Kegan Paul.

Parkin, F. (1971) *Class Inequality and Political Order*, London, Paladin.

Parkin, F. (1979) *Marxism and Class Theory*, London, Tavistock.

Parsons, T. (1965) [1969] 'Full citizenship for the negro American?' In his *Politics and Social Structure*, New York, Free Press.

Pen, J. (1974) *Income Distribution*, Harmondsworth, Penguin.

Poggi, G. (1978) *The Development of the Modern State*, London, Hutchinson.

Sinfield, A. (1978) 'Analyses in the social division of welfare'. *Journal of Social Policy*, 7.

Stephens, J. D. (1979) *The Transition from Capitalism to Socialism*. London, Macmillan.

Thane, P. (1978) Introduction. In P. Thane (ed.) *The Origins of British Social Policy*, London, Croom Helm.

Thane, P. (1978a) 'Non-contributory vs insurance pensions 1878–1908'. In P. Thane (ed.) *The Origins of British Social Policy*, London, Croom Helm.

Thane, P. (1982) *The Foundations of the Welfare State*, London, Longmans.

Therborn, G. (1977) 'The rule of capital and the rise of democracy'. *New Left Review*, No. 103.

Titmuss, R. M. (1958) 'The social division of welfare'. In his *Essays on the Welfare State*, London, Allen and Unwin.

Titmuss, R. M. (1959) 'Health'. In M. Ginsberg (ed.) *Law and Opinion in England in the Twentieth Century*, London, Stevens and Sons.

Touraine, A. (1977) *The Self-Production of Society*, Chicago, University of Chicago Press.

Trotsky, L. (1925) [1973] 'Where is Britain going?'. In *Leon Trotsky on Britain*, New York, Monad Press.

Turner, B. S. (1986) *Citizenship and Capitalism*, London, Allen and Unwin.

Unger, R. M. (1976) *Law in Modern Society*, New York, Free Press.

Weber, M. (1921) [1978] *Economy and Society*, Berkeley, University of California Press.

Weber, M. (1925) [1981] *General Economic History*, New Brunswick, Transaction Books.

Wood, E. M. (1986) *The Retreat from Class*, London, Verso.

Wootton, B. (1955) *The Social Foundations of Wages Policy*, London, George Allen and Unwin.
Young, N. (1967) 'Prometheans or troglodytes? The English working class and the dialectics of incorporation'. *Berkeley Journal of Sociology*, vol. 12.

Index